T0268281

FEELING LEEDS

Raiford Guins

FEELING LEEDS

NOTES ON
LOVING A FOOTBALL
CLUB FROM AFAR

GB

First published by Pitch Publishing, 2022

Pitch Publishing
9 Donnington Park,
85 Birdham Road,
Chichester,
West Sussex,
PO20 7AJ
www.pitchpublishing.co.uk
info@pitchpublishing.co.uk

ISBN 978 1 80150 184 2

Typesetting and origination by Pitch Publishing
Printed and bound in Great Britain by TJ Books, Padstow

Contents

To my son, Deck, for making
the journey with me – until the
world stops going round.

'Importantly, even what is kept at a distance must still be proximate enough if it is to make or leave an impression.'

Sara Ahmed

Acknowledgements

I AM deeply indebted to the following people for their encouragement and guidance across the writing of this book: Henry Lowood, Carlin Wing, Walter Gantz, Rebecca Barden, Charlotte Croft, Phil Rigaud, Tony Atkins, Ellis Cashmore, Matt Knopp, Joanne Forchas and Ian Kimbrey.

I wish to also thank Jane Camillin, Graham Hales, and Gareth Davis at Pitch Publishing for all of their support and assistance with this project. Shout out to Duncan Olner for designing a brilliant book cover!

Special thanks to Omayra Cruz for her patience and ability to listen to so many false starts and half-baked ideas. I am eternally grateful for your belief in my ability (and need) to write this book.

Saturday, 3pm, somewhere

I HAVE invested over $90,000 in Leeds United Football Club. My contribution wasn't covered by Sky Sports, ESPN, or any newspaper. I do not sit on the board of directors. And I do not own any equity shares in the club. A 'foreign' takeover isn't likely. I am neither celebrity fan nor ex-player. I've only visited Switzerland, never opened a bank account there. My assets aren't held offshore. I can also assure you that I am not an oligarch, part of a royal bloodline, or a billionaire investor. If I were a money-spinner, that amount would be mere pocket change, hardly worth these words.

Who am I? Nobody. One of the many global nobodies who supports a football club thousands of miles away from its home ground, town, city, even country. I'm the somnolent supporter who arises at stupid o'clock each Saturday morning (or Sunday) to follow my club. The $90,000 (plus interest) reflects my student loan to attend the University of Leeds in the 1990s. It was a sound investment to diversify my supporter portfolio, if a costly way to close the distance between myself and Leeds United.

The University of Leeds tendered a zone of contact. It meant that I, with international student visa in hand, would finally be there in Leeds, at Elland Road. Not for a one-off match, another tourist jaunt, but for the long haul. Back in 1994 I envisioned this acceptance as a one-way ticket. Life's rhythm tuned into regularly walking down the long, wide steps of Beeston Hill to the ground, buying a chip butty from a food van, selecting tiny enamel football badges outside the ground, and quickly grabbing a copy of the match program along with a fanzine (*The Square Ball*). The mounting elation of kick-off compelled a squeeze into ageing turnstiles to ascend the eminent concrete steps of the Don Revie Stand. I was finally there, unremittingly among the routines, rituals, habits, and superstitious behaviours, all the ordinary, taken-for-granted, sensual and social things people do and experience at a football match. I wished to dwell within this place evermore.

Finally 'being there' was a culmination of years of support, a personal decision to leave friends and family for a career path without guarantee, not to mention accumulate sizeable debt, all in order to experience the everyday intensities of supporting Leeds United: to feel closer to, be a part of, the club I love. This love affair is far from destined. I was neither born into the club via a family line of support nor born in Leeds, neighbouring towns and villages across West Yorkshire, or even in England. I'm from the States. Leeds is a big club with global support, so this fact shouldn't surprise in the least.

What may are the lengths those of us who aren't local, born and bred, or in the same country as our beloved club will go to culture a meaningful connection, a sense of belonging.

A recent article on the 'future fan' in *The Guardian* by Paul MacInnes touches on the question of 'being there' via a different register that nevertheless resounds within this book. The majority of fans, MacInnes reports, 'no longer watch football live in person but digitally through a screen'. This isn't to slight either group, only to note the shifting cartography of football supporters. A polarity has arisen between 'legacy fans' who go to football regularly and so-called 'digital fans' – or the more derisive term, 'Twitter fans'.

The nature of supporting a club has changed, and this emergent demographic of 'digital fans' has prompted clubs – and all fans – to rethink the nature of 'support' and 'engagement'. Is a 'thumbs-up' emoji on Facebook less of a show of support than a scarf swung overhead at Elland Road? Is the sinewy shoulder push of a squeaky turnstile surpassed by the typing of a tweet? Is playing *FIFA* online a form of social interaction on a par with travelling to away matches? It's neither a matter of deciding answers to these off-the-cuff questions nor choosing a side, as it were, but to acknowledge that *how* and *where* many support football, or identify with a club, is being reworked, redefined, experienced diversely. Today, supporters the world over are simultaneously local and distributed. Some *go* to a match; many more *switch it on*.

I can't say that I embrace being lumped into the category of 'digital fan' because of my location, which Google Maps tells me is 3,911 miles from Elland Road. I bump up against it out of necessity rather than choice. Supporting a club from a vast distance isn't a new phenomenon, as anyone crammed into a British pub Stateside for an early morning kick-off in the 1980s and 1990s will affirm. Sky didn't invent football as per the popular maxim, and many across the pond, like me, were watching the English game well before 1992. The difference today, of course, is one of scale. More watch, beyond the seating capacity of any ground. On the flipside, I wish that I could embody the status of 'legacy fans' and go to matches on a regular basis as I once did. This category I long to embrace out of choice but cannot because of economic necessity. To the tune of *Trainspotting*'s opening riff: I chose a job, career, mortgage, family, my son's college fund, insurance, car payments, hotel and airfare costs; life's expenditures a cruel reality, grounding my many flights of fancy. I chose life, just not where I wanted to live it.

I cannot inhabit the label of 'legacy fan', yet I do not neatly fit into the 'digital fan' label either. I'm not convinced that the two categories are mutually exclusive, so I will share what I have done and continue to do to show support and feel connected when 'being there' is more dream than reality. This short book is my attempt to reconcile the practices of passion in the absence of place while acknowledging the reliance on different modes of interaction across 30 years of supporting Leeds United: when ringing the ground for midweek results was the means to acquire news before the internet made such information readily available, when out-of-date copies of *Shoot!* and *Match* plucked from a newsstand became a lifeline to events transpired and the raw material for working out league tables with pen and paper, or when jumping up and down madly while pumping gas as I watched Leeds beat Villa away 3-2 on my iPhone on 23 December 2018 (to the bewilderment of rednecks at the southern Georgia gas station I stopped at when travelling to Tampa, Florida, for Christmas, a sunny pitstop on my way to a Boxing Day match at Elland Road).

Moments like these, travailing for immediacy, along with many more detailed in the book, may seem superfluous to the supporter who can walk, train, or bus to the ground, but those of us with an ocean or continent between ourselves and the turnstiles rely on an assortment of objects, practices, attitudes, and sacrifices to build and sustain our lived – if remote – complex experience of conveying and mediating our support: intimacy through frequent flyer miles, international postage, and the internet. Without the benefit of attending matches routinely across my life, I have had to fill that void with other ways of generating a feeling of belonging. I'm certainly not alone. There are a lot of us out there, strung across the globe. Many attend live matches only a few times a year or never actually visit the home ground of the club they support.

Supporters in these circumstances cannot experience the same sense of belonging that Nick Hornby relishes towards the end of *Fever Pitch* when declaring that Arsenal's victory over Liverpool at the 1987 League Cup 'belonged to me every bit as much as it belonged to Charlie Nicholas and George Graham' on account of the author putting in 'more hours, more years, more decades than them'. My time invested and disparate ways of supporting suggests a different sense of belonging – one nonetheless meaningful but conditioned by the reality of distance – and this book is an attempt to share that difference. It peers into the peculiar and neglected world of the dislocated supporter, the fan who follows a football club devotedly and passionately from afar.

Belonging by place

Why does 'being there' matter? Tony Rickson's *Football Is Better With Fans* sets a scene familiar to many. Matchday, he says, '[Is] about meeting up with friends for a pie and a pint, walking the last bit before going inside the stadium, and getting a first breathtaking glimpse of the magically green grass. Then there's the work to be done. Clapping the players as they come out to warm up and cheering them all over again when they emerge for the match itself. And the following 90 minutes of breathless, heart-warming action. The singing, the chanting, the drama, the experience, the celebrations, the passion. Being a part of it; the warm tingle of camaraderie.'

To help capture this experience for my son and I, our most recently attended match being against Norwich on 13 March 2022, you'd have to add a transatlantic flight, memberships renewed each year for little actual usage, hotel and train bookings, advance planning to coordinate his school and my teaching schedules, the challenge of actually obtaining tickets now that we are back in the Premier League, and, perhaps most important, saving money to actually indulge in that 'warm tingle of camaraderie' (even if only infrequently).

Why bother? Seems like a lot of hassle for 90 minutes, right? It's certainly easier to watch via the numerous apps now available in the US that carry Premier League matches, such as Peacock or fuboTV. In-depth pre-match commentary followed by match reactions are readily available across a range of social media outlets, such as Leeds United Live for example. In fact, I can absorb so many reactions during and after a match via the likes of Twitter, Facebook, Instagram, TikTok and YouTube that I feel bloated by the range of differing opinions. Too much banter, stats, highlight clips, and passion in my diet. What lacks is my own perspective, one that can only be had from the stands.

I will confess to the reader that I place profound value and meaning on being at matches. That's precisely why I went into debt; the reward not financial but cultural, to be privy to the experience of home and away matches. Such proximity is no longer mine to enjoy at ease. So why continue to romanticise it – to plan, save, long, and live for it? A line from Rita Felski's *Hooked: Art and Attachment*, a book not devoted to football but that studies how we connect with and attune ourselves to the things we admire, helps explain my preference for 'being there'. Shunning the long-standing western philosophical position that judgment and criticism requires a removed evaluation, or discerning detachment, she proffers a different direction, 'Distance is not always better than closeness: the bird's-eye view will miss crucial details and telling anomalies; it may result in knowing less rather than more.' Being at a match provides a view that is not universal like the one shared via cameras for television spectators, one that covers only a tiny corner of the pitch to show the on-ball action. But the camera view doesn't capture everything encountered and felt going to the match and walking back, stewing over a poor result or splashing pints in victory.

My view in the stands is subjective. Mine. It has a distinct angle, story, feel, flavour, and smell. It is my experience of being there. The view is obstructed by another supporter's head, arm, or outstretched scarf. It impatiently observes build-up. The beginning of a run not captured on the ball-focused camera. It glances up in disbelief at a missed chance, glances down at my trainers in disgust when scored against. It jostles, jumps, shakes, and quakes when the back of the net is struck. It captures my son tearing up after Norwich's equaliser. It's clouded by tears when we make it 2-1. Unable to control my relief, my joy of being back to witness – after a two-year hiatus – this moment proves overwhelming, raw, hysterical.

It embraces strangers in jubilation. It looks at my son to smile, hug, and dance up and down tumultuously when Joe Gelhardt scores *that* winning goal against the Canaries. We punch the air in chorus to the Kaiser Chiefs' 'I Predict a Riot', raucously applauding the players' grit and determination after the match. This exemplifies the 'rush of togetherness', the collective song of support (the emotional effect of the voice captured elegantly in Simon Critchley's *What We Think About When We Think of Football*).

The angle from the stands isn't just the intense rush but an indicator of the banal, the tiny details missed in such celebratory moments. For instance, being there to have a supporter sat next to my son spy his Adidas trainers as bodies depart for the half, 'Stockholms, flippin 'eck, where did you get those?' The two struck up a conversation. Deck, ten years old, talked to a fellow supporter probably 40 years his senior, explaining that his dad couldn't find his size (UK 12) in shops while he casually strolled into The Hip Store off Vicar Lane the day before the match to find his (UK 7) in stock. Deck got one over on me, he proudly boasted to the bemusement of his friendly inquisitor. The supporter's comment affirmed our presence at the match. It was one instance of the minutia of being there: intimacy of place, the presence of fullness, richness, pure feeling.

In the foreword to Steve Leach's excellent *Twenty Football Towns*, David Cooper, co-director of Manchester Metropolitan's Centre for Place Writing, claims that many books on football like *Fever Pitch* and Tim Park's *A Season with Verona* 'interrogate what it means to steadfastly support *a* team that is rooted in *a* particular place. In different ways, therefore, both books are concerned with the assertion of what might be described as authentic insiderness.'

Leach's book is much more 'promiscuous' in sharing his tales of match-going across multiple clubs and their towns. Being there, for Cooper, helps the supporter 'break out of bubbles of isolation, if only for the afternoon or evening, and experience place as part of a collective'. Simon Critchley shares this conviction, though his word of choice is 'enchantment' to best capture when we are 'lifted out of the everyday into something ecstatic, evanescent and shared, a subtly transfigured sensorium'.

While I appreciate such sentiments, my isolation cannot be measured in afternoons or evenings. More like months. 'Insiderness' eludes. Unless a four-year span of living in Leeds constitutes such a quality? Such status, in my mind at least, isn't one to defend or escalate. It simply points to a different mode of engagement and other types of experiences. Trying to position this form of support, its endurance in particular, requires new language, neither insider nor outsider, 'legacy' nor 'Twitter'. Dislocation seems fitting to describe my personal relationship to Leeds United. Unlike Leach's, I cannot describe my book as 'place writing' but as 'displaced writing'. If 'place matters', and I believe wholeheartedly that it does, then I say that 'displacement matters too' – a desire to feel part of a place and community when proximity fails.

'Being there' supplies the 'crucial details and telling anomalies' of support, the magical stuff, the experiences for attaching ourselves to the club that come from being close, though more often than not lived at distance. These sensations cannot be had when watching remotely. Our view is restricted, fixed for us by the 'bird's eye', not subject to intoxicating, erratic chatter and clutter of life happening en route to the match, outside and inside the ground, and on the mile-and-half walk back to our hotel, when we try desperately to squeeze out as much of that feeling of being within the 'collective' amid the muted sounds of gummy-soled trainers departing. Obtaining, occupying, owning our view in and from the stands places me and Deck in the ground, with and among supporters at Elland Road. Prepositions like 'in', 'with', and 'at' orient me *to* the world of Leeds United, a monogamous affair. The trouble is, when not there, I have to work much harder to replicate this orienting perspective, stretch it out, find ways for it to endure.

Belonging by practice

If place is a profound, though irregular, means of belonging what do I do in the months – years – in between? Life becomes ongoing efforts of re-enchantment, enactment through practices. Permit a little context. One reason for writing this book grew out of my vexed relationship to the profusion of football writing, many exemplars already mentioned above, devoted to personal, evocative narratives on football culture and individual clubs. Not that I dislike such books. In fact, the opposite is the case. I *envy* them.

I long after their collective histories: acts of reflection and remembrance, the exquisite portraits their words paint of standing on terraces, walking to a match, away days, collecting match programmes, attending evening matches played under floodlights, or being at a cup final. In every *Fever Pitch*; *Going To The Match*; *Twenty Football Towns*; *The Quiet Fan*; *What We Think About When We Think About Football*; *32 Programmes*; *Saturday, 3pm*; and *Black Boots & Football Pinks* that I read, my years of support, memories, experiences are absent. They do not, cannot, reside within these pages, though I wish they did. While some memories are shared from my time in England (e.g. Ceefax results, away matches, even a cup final), others appear out of reach. The Englishness of the authors, their 'insiderness', be it by country, place, past, imagined community, or shared social history, removes those histories, experiences, and encounters from the practices of others whose alarm clock ringing just before 7am Eastern (or 4am West Coast) serves as the official's whistle for a UK 'lunchtime' kick-off.

Like Nick Hornby, I did move closer to the club's ground, swapping countries along the way. Unlike Simon Critchley, though, I cannot claim a familial line or reminisce of boyhood heroes like Bill Shankly though I certainly do share his non-neutral perspective when it comes to writing about a beloved club. My support, as you will learn, is accidental, not familial. Unlike Daniel

Gray, I cannot claim the same collective identity he does so easily when declaring, at the outset in *Black Boots & Football Pinks*, 'I am marked by a desire to record what is gone, the consequences of which is the book. I wish to preserve in words the relics of our identity.'

Gray's 'our' doesn't fit me or many others like myself who possess a strong, committed, abiding, 'non-indigenous' history of English football. After all, football is a world sport, and I want to see myself within that world. Our sense of recollection is indirect and complicated, multi-mediated, taking the form of worn VHS copies of *The 1992 Tennants FA Charity Shield: Leeds United v Liverpool*, a bucket hat acquired via mail order from the club, or a scarf gifted to me in 1975. Our recording of events 'gone' looks noticeably different, as the global context of support tosses up other instances, other things used to express love, actions for remembrance, and feelings held from distance. Though different and distant, we still share passion, desire, and deep feeling for the clubs we support. The question of 'how' animates this book. I cannot write books like those of Critchley or Gray. I can only share other experiences and encounters hopefully familiar to many more than the 37,890 that can squeeze into Elland Road on any given matchday.

My shared views rely less on match attendance (or tweets) than on a recording of my encounters with objects, conveyance of experiences and practices cutting across many decades of following Leeds United. It elucidates the 'stuff' I use and do to feel a sense of belonging. In this book, objects, like scarves, badges, or even videocassettes, are deemed magical: they are imbued with qualities and values beyond their intentional functionality. An official club membership card, sticker, 7-inch record, or copy of the *Yorkshire Evening Post* are more than mere things. As with Steven Connor's description of 'magical things' from *Paraphernalia*, they are 'things that we allow and expect to do things back to us'. They are to be 'conjured with, though their magic is done on ourselves rather than others'. These ordinary-cum-magical things are, in the words of another conjuror, Sherry Turkle, 'evocative objects'. They are 'companions in life experience' (greeting me each morning as I welcome the day, slowly drinking coffee from my David Batty mug) heightened in their properties, abilities to emotionally connect, orient me to the world of Leeds United. They keep me in touch. The ordinary objects, habits, routines, hang-ups, peculiarities, and incidental details within these pages are my ways of feeling Leeds. The ordinary, Kathleen Stewart insists in *Ordinary Affect*, 'is a circuit that's always tuned in to some little something somewhere'. I hope that the moments and practices expressed will resonate with other supporters scattered far and wide, celebrating, communicating our shared passion, and varying 'somewheres'. I have tried to texture the labour of support across these pages for those for whom the normal act of watching football is anything but and dislocation defines more than regional accent. It is written by a fan who cannot always be there.

The other reason for writing this book is temporal. For many, the Covid-19 pandemic spurred self-reflection – the occasion to step back from routine and rethink how life is lived, or perhaps can be lived anew once the mask is finally removed. Orange Juice's 'Rip It Up' (and start again) played on regular rotation in my house during 2020. The pandemic proved a moment when *all* supporters became dislocated. Locked out. Locked down. Distanced from their clubs.

This universal dislocation – stinging even more as it was our championship season – prompted me to reflect on my decades of support and sense of self *as* a supporter. With shop shelves empty, toilet roll stockpiled, and cargo ships held outside harbours, time seemed the only commodity in abundance. I used it to look at my own ways of supporting. Writing itself proved emotionally vital during this period, a precious and available means to feeling closer through exposition: committing words to illuminate my practices and experience of support, brief encounters with my efforts, tireless as they are, to orient myself nearer. For large chunks of time during lockdown, the only place I could travel was to the forlorn blank page (a journey with its own peril), a portal to the outside world.

My life has often felt like a series of misses, events just beyond the reach of a goalkeeper's fingertips. I missed being a native Californian by a few months. I missed a riotous period of music (1977–1982) by being born a little too late. Record collecting is the costly means to subvert that misfortune. I caught the tail end of the Howard

27

Wilkinson era but left Leeds just before David O'Leary's babes blossomed. I refused to miss this opportunity, even if steeped in the prolonged disappointment, disarray, and death wrought by a pandemic. In the vein of many bands who socially distanced in their studios to produce pandemic recordings, this book is my cathartic jam session: a concept album about distance and my personal efforts to collapse it.

1

Beeston Hill, 1993

TYPICAL TOURIST move. I arrived at Leeds station and approached an information kiosk for accommodation. B&B or hotel; whichever was cheapest would do. It was my first visit to the city to attend my first match at Elland Road. A friendly back-and-forth with the two men working the kiosk – supporters of course – on the eve of our first home match of the new 1993/94 season yielded directions to a mate's B&B in a place called Beeston. It's walkable to Elland Road, he said. Sold.

On my walk to Elland Road from Beeston, I skirted Holbeck Cemetery. It was my first real look at the famous ground, since the brief peek through a dirty train window en route from King's Cross lacked romance. Unbeknownst to me at the time, I trod respectfully through the same area that Tony Harrison eulogises while visiting his parents' grave in his poem *v.* The film version shown on Channel 4 launches with Harrison standing graveside directing the camera in opposite directions: pointing at the viewer, he motions towards, 'Town Hall, Leeds Grammar school, and University of Leeds where I studied, got the education that took me away from this background,' and then shares the view that overlooks Elland Road. I study this footage solemnly. Not just as a prelude to *v.* but often isolated from the poem. The poet's personal bearings speak to me.

In Beeston for football, the view towards Elland Road was all that mattered. The other view, towards the University of Leeds, was not yet in focus. I walked down the long steps of Beeston Hill. 'Walking to the ground', as the expression goes, is a time-honoured hallmark of football support. A social experience immortalised in L.S. Lowry's 1953 painting *Going to the Match*, now in the possession of the Professional Footballers' Association. Hard to experience this sensation, this rite of passage, for the dislocated when driving a car to a pub, switching on a television, or watching via a smartphone is how many 'go' to the match these days. Walking was how I had long imagined my first trip to Elland Road, each step closing time and distance to the match, connecting me to the tradition of the club and all the supporters who walked before me. Taxi or bus would hardly do.

I had to arrive by my own means of locomotion, feet stepping across an unfamiliar soil. Rudimentary awareness. Walking allows us to set the pace. To step briskly, if running late, or desultorily, should time lack importance. Walking allows us to move among the environment outside transport that shields our senses. By doing so, we observe the overlooked, or that which is skewed from view by a faster, perfunctory tempo.

We feel the ground on which we tread. We dirty, scuff our shoes, the environment reminding us of its blunt presence. Walking to Elland Road allowed me a sense of ordinariness, one foreign to my status as a first-time visitor from afar; I was temporarily pinpointed on a map, primed to make my first impression upon those long steps.

My direction known. Breathed in. Onward, towards the kaleidoscopic culture of football. The sights and sounds of Elland Road pulling me closer. Offering the most sublime view. Not one lifting me above the crowd, but clasping me in its frenzied, intimate rhythm. Compelling a quickened pace, still absorbing the scene of matchday with bodies scurrying, pulses racing, smells, many unidentifiable, wafting from food trucks. I'd walk down those long steps of Beeston on other days, non-matchdays. They are exactly that, ordinary cement steps, but for a few hours, they transform. On each matchday, the steps from Beeston Hill are imbued with meaning, custom, and function.

My desire to experience 'going to the match' on foot was a reality. I occupied Harrison's dual perspectives, with one eye on Elland Road and the other affixed on the University of Leeds, where I would eventually study. Where Harrison was taken from his background, I was taken to a football ground and a future. The differing views from Holbeck Cemetery aligned perfectly: *et augebitur scientia* ('and knowledge will be increased', the motto of the University of Leeds) *and* football at Elland Road. Where the dead rested, I began to live.

2

'Why did you come to Leeds?'

MY FIRST match, on 7 August 1993, proved decisive. It demonstrated not only that one could purchase a plane ticket using the proceeds from sperm donation, as I had, but more importantly that an application to the University of Leeds was a potential path to making Elland Road and Leeds United part of my everyday life rather than a rare occasion.

Academia seemed the best option. I had long since internalised the lyrics of The Clash's 'I'm So Bored with the USA', followed by The Exploited's 'Fuck the USA'. Other means of emigration appeared unrealistic: sports (I only returned to Sunday league competitive football in my 30s), music (punk didn't pay back then, or was only starting to for the likes of Green Day), or the military (I saw the Marine Corps chew up and spit out my father's body in the name of duty, so no thanks). To play it safe, I applied widely to programs in the UK just in case an offer from Leeds failed to arrive. When the acceptance letter – yes, a piece of paper – from the University of Leeds appeared in my physical mailbox, the decision was made. Season tickets, soon to hand.

And so I arrived, a newly minted postgraduate at the University of Leeds. During the first seminar for incoming MA students pursuing degrees in social art history, feminist art history, or, in my case, cultural studies, Professor Griselda Pollock called on each of us to share our personal reasons for pursing graduate studies at Leeds or, as she phrased it, why we chose to partake in the 'Leeds project'. Students shared their research interests, projects committed to politics, history, and theory and, in particular, projects informed deeply by Griselda's foundational work in feminist art history, along with the scholarship of the social historians of art Fred Orton and Adrian Rifkin, both slouched against the wall because of a lack of seating.

I immediately felt like an imposter. Being at the University of Leeds to support a football club felt like a betrayal to students serious in their intellectual pursuits. I started to feel unworthy of being in the room. A joke. An idiot. An embezzler misappropriating my student loan on football, stealing from another person denied a place on a degree on account of my acceptance. Neither overcommitted to politics, nor possessing any interest in 'fine art' (unless you count Tony Yeboah's uncanny volley against Liverpool in 1995, which I was privileged to witness from the Revie Stand). I grew anxious as my turn grew closer with each thoughtful and profound response.

As it happens, cultural studies was a natural fit for me. I was and remain fascinated by cultural history. In learning more about the field prior to my departure to Leeds, I was immediately struck by what I dubbed the 'Leeds connection' between Richard Hoggart, who grew up in Hunslet and studied English at the University of Leeds, and E.P. Thompson, who taught in the university's extra-mural department. Both figures loom large in the history of cultural studies for their groundbreaking books *The Uses of Literacy* and *The Making of the English Working Class*.

Although football features little – no more than a few lines – in Hoggart's account of northern working-class culture, I always imagined that he supported Leeds United, growing up such a short distance from Beeston. I hoped as well that Thompson's time in Leeds induced a soft spot towards the club. I still smile when I teach Thompson's critique of Raymond Williams's *The Long Revolution* to graduate students in the US as they struggle with his football metaphor that includes Marx, Weber, and Mannheim as part of a 'very different eleven of Players fielding against' Williams's reliance on the literary tradition of T. S. Eliot and Matthew Arnold.

If the likes of Hoggart and Thompson – innovative in their thoughts and methods – could reference football in their respected works, would it not be fitting for football to be a catalyst for attending the University of Leeds? These writers made everyday life and culture their subjects of research, and I was in Leeds to experience the ordinariness of supporting a local club: walking to the ground when Saturday comes, freezing during winter midweek matches, reading the *Yorkshire Evening Post* on buses, nitpicking over matches in cafes and pubs with fellow supporters. The University of Leeds was my phenomenological instrument to get closer to these experiences.

'Thank you, next.' The dreaded words from Griselda, passing the dealer's shoe in my direction. Throat cleared. Legs shaking. Head beginning to lift. Whetting of lips to speak.

'I support Leeds United.'

Before I could rush to qualify my truth with more legitimate gravitas – 'and to do British cultural studies by studying at an institution so important to the field's history' – Griselda surprised me and the many disciples planted at her feet, 'I support Leeds as well. We must go to a match together sometime.'

Silence. Disbelief smacked across my face and the faces of those in attendance. 'Really?' was all I could muster. The most significant art historian of her generation, one who practically invented feminist art history, not only followed Leeds United but also went to matches with her son regularly.

An immediate connection was established between us. It remains to this day. We never did attend a match together. Griselda sat with her son and husband in the family stand while I found my place in the Revie Stand. Our paths did cross now and again. Travelling to Wembley for the 1996 League Cup Final, the supporters' bus I was on stopped at one of those nondescript motorway service areas on the M1. As I reached for a newspaper inside the shop, my hand made contact with another. The hand pulled back to reveal its owner: Griselda.

'Ray!'

'Griselda!'

We hugged. Excited, joyful, and full of hope for the final. After being humiliated by Villa, we didn't even need to exchange words when back in the department on Monday. The knowing look of disappointment, the sighs shared, was enough commiseration. 'Wilko Out' was the headline soon after.

Leeds United remains a topic of fervent conversation whenever I see Griselda, whether on the occasion of her lecture at the prestigious Hammer Museum in Los Angeles or when I'm back in the city for a match. On the emotional day of winning the Championship title on 18 July 2020, my inbox overflowed with messages from friends sending their congratulations. I spied one that read simply 'Promotion!!!!' It was from Griselda. 'Are you jumping for joy. Leeds got promoted!!! … 18 years loyalty for my son. I thought of you.' That day brought so many of us together despite the pandemic contriving to keep us apart. I printed Griselda's email, a souvenir of our friendship. I remain truly touched. Here is an exceptional, world-class scholar, one who has been awarded not one but two honourary doctorates, has held numerous chair and director roles, has authored too many books and articles to list in this space, taking time out from her always exhausting schedule to share the joy of Leeds' promotion back to the Premier League with her former student from over 20 years ago.

3

Scarf: 1975

THE SCARF has a long history of distinguishing its wearer's status, rank, or affiliation. Its history goes something like this: a silk scarf first appeared around the long, slender neck of Queen Nefertiti of Egypt in 1300BC, while cloth versions signalled military rank during the reign of Emperor Chang (33–7BC) as part of the Han dynasty. Sourced materials, silk and cotton, were used to connote class status, as 17th-century Croatian soldiers marked high-ranking officers with silk and those of lesser rank with cotton. This association continued. The 19th century witnessed Queen Victoria adorn silk scarves as a signature of nobility, while later, at the crack of the 20th century's dawn, many crocheted long, khaki-coloured wool scarves to honour the bravery of British servicemen during the Second Boer War.

Scarves became fashion accessories, with the French company Hermès being the first to produce ready-to-wear, graphically adorned luxury silk scarves in the late 1930s. Academic study, too, inherits this tradition of distinction, most notably with students bedecked in coloured stripes, emanating from colour patterns found on a university or college's coat of arms, running the length of long woollen scarves expressing institutional affiliation – Tom Baker's appearance as The Doctor in *Doctor Who* being an obvious exemplar.

At some point, probably in the early 20th century and ages before the relative newcomer replica team kits – home, away, the cash-grab third strip – were common, the scarf was an inexpensive means of publicly displaying one's support. The 'football scarf' or 'supporter's scarf', originally hand-knitted in the form of 'granny scarves', slotted in among other visual markers such as ribbon rosettes, coloured hats, and wooden rattles hand-painted in a club's colours. The scarf is surely *the* most enduring marker of a supporter's allegiance. It is said to have debuted in England, with practicality part and parcel to its adoption, specifically warmth – though such adherence to functionality falls away when scarves are stretched over a head, tied around a wrist, pulled through a belt loop, twirled rapidly, and spied in the sweltering heat of summer cup tournaments.

Whether as souvenir, protection from the elements, or signifier for self and club identity, the scarf is an extraordinary thing. Unlike pennants, scarves aren't purchased to stay at home on a wall, though some do find their way there. Scarves travel with us. Unlike programs, they aren't filed away. Like a shirt, they are worn. But one doesn't outgrow a scarf. It isn't given over to fading and shrinkage like garments tossed in a wash cycle. A scarf doesn't show armpit stains. The scarf abides: holding its form even when twirled and stretched; splotches – be they tea, sweat, maybe blood, or just general grime – add to the scarf's charisma and fuzzy patina in ways that chip grease or beer stains down the front of one's white home kit never will. The scarf swaddles its wearer. Intimately. Lovingly. It's worn during the highs, whipping the air with each euphoric twirl, and the lows, when the scarf becomes a security blanket clinched tightly to our face. The football scarf is a deeply, profoundly personal thing: a constant presence to its wearer – knotted just so to dance across one's chest – and to onlookers, shouting, 'We Are Leeds'.

My first Leeds scarf came not in accordance with acts of valour on the battlefield but in the form of a Christmas gift in 1975. I cannot say that I was thrilled about receiving such a present. It was a far cry from the coveted *Star Trek* USS Enterprise action playset with realistic 'transporter' (a spinning triangular shaft that once spun hid, i.e. 'dematerialised', *Star Trek* figures). Yet when advised that my aunt had purchased the scarf while on holiday in Paris earlier that year, I took notice. I didn't know what the weird name, 'Leeds United', printed on the white with thin blue stripes meant. 'United' against what? What is 'Leeds'? I didn't think to ask where. I was five years old. Google Maps didn't exist. All I knew was that it was a football scarf. My aunt was told when she purchased it that Leeds United was a great English soccer team. I received it as a gift because of my interest in the sport. I was, after all, one of Pelé's so-called 'children' learning to play in the 1970s at the height of the NASL. My knowledge of Leeds United grew somewhat, though by no massive leaps and bounds. I wore the scarf to a Washington Diplomats match, my local club at the time, at Robert F. Kennedy Memorial Stadium in the late 1970s (when Johan Cruyff played for the Dips). A few Brits commented on my scarf, though I'd be lying if I said I remember what they said. I imagine that 'Super Leeds' rang out.

The scarf is still in my possession. It's my most beloved object. The old adage that you 'never forget your first' holds true even for microfibres. For Leeds supporters, 'Paris 75' is bitter, riotous. I won't rehash the public record on *that* European Cup Final here. 'We are the champions, champions of Europe' full stop. What haunts me is that my aunt was in Paris around the time of the match and bought me a Leeds United scarf – because, as she was told, they are a great English soccer team. I'm connected to that moment despite being oblivious at the time.

My aunt, Shirley Alexiou, passed away from liver cancer in 2010. When I recently contacted my uncle to confirm the exact dates of the trip, he responded, 'I have difficulty remembering what I had for breakfast,' so pinning down any more details on my scarf's history is unlikely. The thought that my gift may have been a Bayern Munich scarf has crossed my mind, making *this* book improbable. My decades of supporting Leeds United is an accident of commitment, the existential choice I make again and again.

I cannot claim that my support for Leeds began in 1975. If anything, it was the awakening of an affinity realised much later. I will say, in retrospect, that my life lived since has filled in the tiny holes of my mysterious Christmas gift's frayed cotton by making those then-unknown words eventually significant. My scarf accrued meaning over time. It enacted something. I've dedicated large chunks of my life to that gift, reciprocated not to its bringer, though I'm sure she received a hug, but to the club of which the name is inscribed upon it. A loving aunt's thoughts of her young nephew brought me inadvertently to Leeds. I'm obliged to follow.

4

Scarf: 1986

UNPACKING IS bittersweet. My practical side just wants to have everything in order as quickly as possible. My sentimental side – which typically wins – lingers over each object to reacquaint myself with its meanings and values. The latter side can be cumbersome, or so my wife often notes. I have moved a lot throughout my life. From 1998 to 2008, I count around ten different moves. Life entailed the constant pursuit of cardboard boxes along with untold amounts of packing tape.

My family moved from Okinawa, Japan to Tampa, Florida, in the summer of 1986. Not only was I forced to leave friends and a place I loved, I missed the entire World Cup in transit. 'Soccer' was not yet dipping so much as a toe into the overcrowded pool of the US sports market in the mid-1980s. The once-popular NASL had folded. World Cup and television coverage of sports other than those played by US teams was resigned to ABC's *Wide World of Sports* on Saturday afternoons. Think about that for a minute – the only televised outlet for non-US based sports consisted of a compilation show that ran for a few hours once a week. The only other television coverage – if you had cable – took the form of Spanish-language regional networks like Telemundo. Unlike Maradona's hand, I missed all the goals for the 1986 World Cup.

In unpacking my personal belongings during that summer, I happened upon my Leeds United scarf from 1975. The tropical climate of Okinawa made the need for it unnecessary, as did my yet to be realised passion. My scarf, along with my sled, went into long-term storage. This requires context. When a member of the US military – my father, in this case – is stationed abroad, a great number of belongings are stored to adhere to weight allowance allotted for relocation. Not only did I have to unpack items that lived with me in Okinawa (wetsuits, body board, records), but I was reunited with possessions stored many years prior. The sentimental experience was overwhelming as items long forgotten were returned *en masse*.

When unpacking boxes marked 'kids' room' – mind, I was now 16 – I expected the odd assortment of old books, comics, and toys abandoned that teenage life had rendered uncool. My Leeds scarf took me completely by surprise. I had just left all of my friends behind, and as The Jam's song goes, I found myself in a strange town. Returning to the US in the mid-1980s was total culture shock: Reaganism, Cola wars, the Iran-Contra hearings, 1950s nostalgia, 'Spuds MacKenzie', and the California Raisins performing in the key of brownface. I immediately rejected this America and further embraced punk rock. Luckily, Tampa had an incredible scene in the 1980s, a safe haven from rednecks and jocks who were not particularly fond of Dead Kennedys or Black Flag T-shirts, let alone any hairstyle that dared to defy the mullet.

I'm tempted to read my embrace of the club at this moment as yet another instance of rejecting America with its star-strangled culture (even the Statue of Liberty got a facelift in 1986). Had that been the case, it's doubtful that my love for the club would endure. I'll grant that the turn to the club fed *l'étranger* status, intentionally alienating me from family, friends, and US culture. Beginning to follow Leeds United felt like sustenance. At the time, Billy Bremner was the club's manager, average attendances at Elland Road were nearly half the stadium's capacity, and the major highlight was a strong FA Cup run in the 1986/87 season. I watched not a single match, relying only on whatever print sources I could lay my hands on to learn of results (usually no more than a league table).

What captured my attention and began knitting a feeling of belonging was the banter at local pubs. Being among other supporters fed the passion, though the rediscovered scarf absolutely whetted the appetite. The thought that Leeds United matches would have been shown via satellite at this time is laughable, of course. Yet football culture itself was alive in the pubs that I frequented. Fans talked of *their* clubs, typically Manchester United, Liverpool, or Rangers. Every now and again, they'd pause to give me stick for donning my

Leeds scarf (especially in Florida). It was all tongue-in-cheek, friendly banter that taught a certain teenager the importance of learning to take a verbal jab (even if always outnumbered). My involvement – sometimes I elicited no more than an 'all right' when taking a seat at the bar or 'why Leeds?' when my club affiliation became a topic for conversation (and derision) – meant that I was starting to be identified *as* a Leeds United supporter. The scarf that set me apart from friends and family, if not all US culture, opened a path to different acquaintances, another national culture to embrace, and eventually a life lived with Leeds woven through.

5

Faded bucket hat, or not being in Bournemouth in 1990

I WISH that my Leeds United bucket hat's faded colours resulted from bank holiday sunshine in May 1990. That weekend lives in the memory of many for two reasons, one being the £1m in damages that ensued from violence between supporters and Dorset police. The other, much more positive of course, was the win over AFC Bournemouth that allowed Leeds United to clinch the 1989/90 Second Division title and return to the First Division after a near-decade absence (sounds familiar, I know). I wasn't among the 4,000 ticket holders or thousands without tickets who made the journey to the south coast. I was stuck in Tampa.

News of the title, on this side of the Atlantic, was sparse to say the least. I visited local British pubs, desperate to secure newspapers covering the title or solicit any bits of first-hand accounts regulars may have received from friends and family back in the UK. I visited my newsstand a month later to purchase copies of *Shoot!* and *Match* to decorate my bedroom walls. And as time moved on, I found myself seated at a library microfiche machine scrolling through news stories covering that weekend. Anything I could lay my hands on offered more clues to the portrait of promotion I was trying desperately to piece together for myself.

A much fuller view eventually presented itself: the club's official videocassette of the title-winning season. Of course, I can now watch my share of footage thanks to YouTube, ranging from Vinnie Jones's pre-match decry that 'Leeds United fans can behave themselves' to club chairman Leslie Silver sharing his position that the Football League ought to have considered rearranging the bank holiday weekend fixture. That moment in the club's history, my first trophy as a Leeds supporter, is stitched together via these media fragments. The biggest puzzle piece is my cherished bucket hat, ordered from the club's shop along with a Second Division champions pendant that still hangs proudly in my university office and that I see as I write this sentence. The bucket hat connects me to that moment more than any other object.

In photos captured over that now-notorious weekend, supporters can be spotted singing shirtless with bucket hats arrayed, a sign of support and summery weather. The bucket hat didn't have much cache in the States at that time; it rather closely resembled lure-ridden fishing hats worn by grandfathers or boonie hats worn by Vietnam vets. Muted colours like khaki or olive were the norm, not a sloping brim emblazoned in blue with 'Leeds United' in bold text wrapping around a white field dotted by sunshine yellow at the crown. My bucket hat, needless to say, raised more than a few eyebrows when worn in the States before the Stone Roses, Ocean Colour Scene, and Oasis made them fashionable worldwide.

My bucket hat is a marker of that moment not directly lived. It places me among the crowd of travelling and jubilant supporters depicted in photos, news reports, and television coverage. I wanted desperately to envision myself there. Its lightweight cotton material is given this heavy burden, to connect two emotional worlds: that of Leeds United supporters celebrating the title on location in Bournemouth, those back in Leeds, and those, like myself, distant and pining for the occasion. We missed the party, but we got a hat. And that is something.

The bucket hat is a highly evocative object for me, second only to my scarf from 1975. It too continues to travel with me. It isn't hidden away in a wardrobe or dresser or stashed in a basement. It's on my hat rack, ready for use, an endearing companion in daily life (though its service as headwear is limited, mainly because either it shrunk from washing or my head grew from Leeds United winning the First Division title a few years later). My hat doesn't provide false testimony. I wasn't there in Bournemouth. What it speaks, however, is support from afar, as evidenced by an ordinary piece of dyed, foldable cloth connecting me to the event.

My bucket hat has featured in my support for over 30 years. This bemuses me. Degrees or certificates, trophies, photo albums, family heirlooms, early childhood toys, or furniture are the more common objects treasured for so long. But a thin, cheap, piece of cloth sewn for one size fits all?

That which is transient is rendered permanent, or at least identified as worthy of an extended lifespan. For the bucket hat still offers some sense of protection beyond shielding me from UVA rays. Having not been able to attend any matches that season (well beyond the meagre budget of a 19-year-old) it bears witness to the period when bucket hats were part and parcel of terrace culture (back *en vogue* again, of course). It dates my long support before the American-style baseball hat became the accepted headwear of English football clubs. It documents another era when one like me would have to scramble from pub to pub to find newspapers, or even consult a microfiche machine – now dumped in library basements – for images deemed priceless. And my bucket hat's odd appearance in the States at the time signalled my own alien status, a sporting other, decipherable only to British expats, who either gave me the 'thumbs up', to acknowledge Leeds United winning the Second Division, or two fingers. Either way, it communicated my support publicly, and for decades now, it has protected my personal memory of the title-winning season.

6

Beans on toast at Scotland Yard, Tampa, FL

TODAY, 9 February 2022, we play away to Aston Villa. The kick-off is at 3pm Eastern Standard Time. Ten minutes before kick-off, I walk downstairs, power up my television and Xbox One X, and initiate the Peacock app, where today's match is streaming live. Beforehand, I check various news sources for today's line-up. But when the match kicks off, I leave to pick up my son from school.

Walking out of the door and into my car, I immediately tap the Peacock app on my iPhone. I then carefully position the phone – one mustn't be distracted while driving. Live match noise replaces music as I cruise to my son's school with the windows down on a mild winter day. I watch intently in the parking lot. Daniel James opens the scoring. I'm bouncing around in my car, shouting, singing, punching its roof. My son walks out. I motion to him quickly, 'C'mon, James just scored, we're one up.' We listen and watch excitedly on the short drive back home. We arrive around 3.25pm, vigorously shed our winter coats, kick off our shoes haphazardly, run riot downstairs to watch on our television. Football travels with us today. I am always within arm's reach of a match. Had this particular match been available via fuboTV, I could have watched on my car's touchscreen.

The late-20th century me would regard the above as pure science fiction, a wonderful future on the horizon, a football fan's hover car of tomorrow. My reality back then was somewhat different. The scene then looked more like this: an early Saturday morning breakfast, swimming in grease, with scalding cups of tea for the rousted on hand to gape fervently at a square box affixed in the corner of a pub. That reality whiffed of sausage and crack of dawn pints. Each week I rang my 'local' pub to inquire about the fixture to be shown Saturday morning via satellite. I underscore 'local', as my weekly journey to the Scotland Yard pub was a 40-minute drive each way. Should a match not be available at Scotland Yard because of a transmission issue, which was common, I travelled further afield to St. Petersburg, Clearwater, Dunedin, or Bradenton. Florida's Bay Area was dotted by British and Irish pubs with picturesque names like Harp and Thistle, King's Head, Rose and Crown, Fox and Hound. They were the only game in town for expats, along with Americans with an appetite for the sport.

Upon arrival at Scotland Yard, once located at 6507 W. Waters Ave, punters would pay an entrance fee of $20 that included the 'match of the day' and a full English breakfast. According to a 1992 issue of *Shoot!*, an average ticket at Elland Road during the 1991/92 season was £17, putting our satellite Saturday seemingly on par with the First Division and, shortly, Premier League ticket prices (for some clubs, at least). Match coverage was prone to interruption or loss of signal at any moment. On some occasions, we wouldn't receive a match at kick-off, joining later in the first half – to the chagrin of sleepy-headed supporters, with an increasingly nervous owner contemplating the spectre of refunds.

The owner in question was Peter 'Wardy' Ward, who played for Brighton & Hove Albion and Nottingham Forest before moving to the NASL and the MISL (Major Indoor Soccer League). If memory serves, he was playing with the Tampa Bay Rowdies while pulling pints at Scotland Yard. My good friend and former professor, Ellis Cashmore, with whom I often watched matches at Scotland Yard and who is certainly no stranger to football culture, clued me into Ward's history. It was common to share space with former or current Tampa Bay Rowdies. The Wegerle brothers – Roy, Geoff and Steve – were spotted often, and I seem to have always missed Rodney Marsh, who 'popped in' just recently.

The space was what one has come to expect at British pubs in the US: Union Jacks and St George flags adorning walls; cluttered if not tawdry pictures of royal figures, the occasional Churchill, the landscape painting drenched in blood sports; an assortment of colourful beer towels like the one's punks used to sew on their jeans; out-of-date British tabloids littering the bar; football scarves, pendants, and jerseys pinned to the walls to fill in the rest of the interior cracks. Traditions like quiz nights and raffles endured. The pub also sponsored a formidable team playing in the Hillsborough County league.

As inelegant as the walls would appear to the outsider, they were a culture that I wanted desperately to drink up. Here I would learn to really watch football, not just to applaud goals but to appreciate how a play builds up, how defenders work an offside trap, the importance of a high defensive line and wingers playing out wide. I also observed the commentary, rivalries displayed over breakfast in a room clouded with cigarette. Results from other matches were always met with a cheer, should one's club have won, or a loud 'bloody hell' should a result go in the opposite direction. No one checked their own mobiles for a result. We had none then. When Ward called out results, noted from a landline phone call, that was as close to 'live streaming' that I got unless Leeds were selected for transmission, which was frustratingly rare, as the television was generally given over to Liverpool, Arsenal, and Manchester United.

At the Scotland Yard, I learned to value and appreciate not only the nuances of football culture, accompanied by the joy of having a Saturday ritual, but the taste of beans on toast. I stopped eating meat in 1987, and that full English shoved at my chest was far from appetising with its ration of bacon and sausage. I observed the practice of drowning one's buttery toast with Heinz Baked

Beanz, pure processed pleasure in an iconic tin. I would experience my first pasty at Elland Road in the mid-1990s when going to home matches regularly. I also warmed to the charming chip butty, accompanied with brown sauce, from a van outside the ground. Football and beans on toast? A perfect combination for breakfast, a tradition kept alive in my family to this day – but never when watching a match in our car. Breakfast not lunch, beans not Bovril, became an associative smell, savour, texture, my *madeleine de Proust*.

7

Mail order supporter

TODAY'S SUPPORTERS have it easy. As a testament to the voracious brand prowess of the Premier League, you can saunter into a Nike or Adidas shop to purchase a strip as easy as you like. Typically, that transaction is open only to select clubs, those that marketing research deems sufficiently high-profile to command space in a shop. In the States, you are more likely to find a Manchester United top than one for the League One side Accrington Stanley, part of the same three-stripe branding family. The same goes for Torquay United and Peterborough United: not only are both clubs quite a few leagues beneath the likes of Chelsea and Spurs, they aren't promoted to the retail floor space at any Nike shop despite sharing the same swoosh. If you can't be bothered to travel to a shop or your club plays in a different league, you needn't worry. Just click to the official online store of your favourite club and load up your cart.

At the risk of veering into crotchety-old-guy territory, let me tell you about what it was like not so long ago, say,

30 years, give or take, when someone like me living outside the UK had to write a letter, place it in an envelope, visit a post office for international (or 'foreign', as they were once known) stamps, and mail off the request. And then wait. For a long time. After faithfully checking the postbox day after day, the magic envelope suddenly appeared. The Royal Mail postmark immediately revealed its secret: a Leeds United club shop catalogue, the means to obtain a scarf, paper-thin flat cap, eight-panel or bucket hat, T-shirt, or pennant.

I would pore over these for hours on end, dog-earing page after page to the point where the glossy paper gave way to matte. I'd carefully place tiny pen marks next to the items I desired. Then I'd carefully fill in the order form. Next came estimating currency exchange – postage from the UK has always been exorbitant – and another trip, this time to a bank for an international money order. The postal effect of anticipation was reignited. And then to wait. For a long time, again. More desperate mailbox checks. More agony. Until arrival. And surprise, the Royal Mail postmark gave away the A2, A3, or A4 small parcel's contents.

Football magazines offered mail-order services to acquire club merchandise as well. Little square ads, typically located in the back of a magazine, were a second commodity lifeline to Leeds United via post. Why extol what sounds like an utter inconvenience compared to the little gold basket – which doesn't really look like a basket but more like a gym bag or purse – located at the upper-right corner of the Leeds United official online shop? One answer is that supporters, serious supporters, had few alternatives prior to online shopping – only trips to sports shops that specialised in football gear, the grounds, or city centre shops prevailed. I think another answer lies in a messy mingling of macho sentimentalism. As Teddy Roosevelt would have it, 'Nothing in the world is worth having or worth doing unless it means effort, pain, difficulty.' The lack of availability coupled with the persistence required to acquire tokens of affection for a club demonstrated devotion in my mind. The more arduous it proved to find Leeds United items, the more meaningful the pursuit, and the more treasured the possession, became.

Mail order, though, was a mysterious enterprise full of chance, risk. The moment my letter left my hand at a post office? One of hope whose collar is sharply tugged back by instant dread. Will it arrive? Will it perform its utilitarian service of monetary exchange for goods? Will it perform its vital emotive service, help me shorten the distance between myself and Leeds United via postal machinery, fulfil the promise of delivery whispered in the moistened application of stamps? I envisioned my letter chafed, crushed, mishandled, deformed by insensitive conveyor belts plotting with the brute cruelty of mechanical arms violently sorting and pushing it through a complex system. I placed my trust in a vast network of people, places, and machines to safely and securely – before packages were tracked, barcoded, scanned – deliver my money and goods across an ocean.

The process heads in my direction: deliver my items, presumably intact, to their final destination, me. Will the sender's parcel reach its recipient, my existence officially acknowledged by the club in the form of my personal address inscribed upon a mailer? Or will it be lost? I felt the sensation of loss each time something failed to make its destination. A feeling of abandonment from the club I admired so. Order forms, torn from the back of catalogues, filled in with pen, felt like love letters dispatched across a great divide in hope that the adored would respond. The return wasn't an adroitly folded letter, tenderly written. It was far more precious: a Second Division champions pennant 1989/90. Well worth the wait.

8

011+44+113, or when Wednesday comes

KARL OVE Knausgård and Fredrik Ekelund's splendid book *Home and Away: Writing the Beautiful Game* concerns reflection – one author spending his summer in Southern Sweden watching the 2014 FIFA World Cup on television, the other in Brazil attending matches, soaking up the scene. They chronicle the event in a daily exchange of ideas, impressions, and inquiries about the sport, the styles of play and players, this particular tournament and those past, the crafts of writing and reading, family and friends, and life (and death) in general. The sport of football is an entry point into worlds for the pair. Though they use the word 'letters', I suspect that the form of writing consisted of words banged out on a keyboard rather than hand to paper.

Their exchanges, especially their ability to comment and critique while watching, soon after, early in the morning, or when tired at night, caused me to circle back in time to when mail or a long-distance phone call connected me with the game. Today, my access to all things Leeds United is effortless. All I require is an internet connection and input device. Each morning, I scroll through articles on the club via the *Yorkshire Evening Post*. The idea of a regional paper feels confused to me these days. I'm a more avid reader of what's happening in Headingley, Holbeck, or Hunslet than of what's in my own backyard. Next, I check out a few fan sites, and by just typing a 'L' into safari on my iPhone, I'm taken to NewsNow, where I scan through rumours. I can rapid-fire my opinions on a match, transfer, or player via Twitter or Facebook (though I rarely do). I can watch my fill of post-match commentary via a variety of streaming services, not to mention match highlights compiled within what seems like seconds of a final touch.

In the late 1980s and 1990s, I followed in fragments, highlights on videocassettes, the odd match at a pub, and league tables sporadically printed in newspapers. To rectify the absence of knowledge, acquire an unknown result, or find out who scored in a match, I dialled a country code (011) and city code (113) into my landline telephone to ring Elland Road directly. Locating the rest of the number required library research into the ground's address and considerable steering through an international operator switchboard. I was often connected to different offices at the ground with various degrees of success. The club shop proved the most reliable. Someone on the other end was always willing to share a result with me, my foreign accent breaking up the monotony of a day on the till.

Midweek results were the most precious, as these never appeared in my local newspaper. I recall ringing the club shop – in the pre-Super Store days – to inquire about a League Cup match. A woman's voice on the other end shared the news, 'The city is a ghost town today. Everyone is just gutted.' We lost by three goals. Against which club? Lost to history. Regardless, our cup run ended. Just to speak to someone about the match directly thrilled me, despite the bad result. Her West Yorkshire accent drew me in. I wanted badly to be in that ghost town, to commiserate with others, to lift each other up for the next match, to tell one another the old alibi that the league is more important than a good cup run.

What struck me about this antiquated practice in the course of reading Knausgård and Ekelund's book was the relationship with the club via telephony. I loathe speaking on a phone. Even today. I answer my phone only to a select few. I much prefer text, email, FaceTime, Zoom, or physical face-to-face interaction. Perhaps it's on account of having to work hard to fill in the missing sensual experience of vision or the demands the phone places on participation between speakers, between the mouth and ear conjoined via handpiece clumsily pressed against a shoulder. Maybe it's the boredom of twiddling the cord or doodling (knowing that the little scribble will never grow into full maturity).

Those calls to Elland Road were the exception. They personified the ancient Greek etymology of 'tele', meaning 'afar' or 'far off', with 'phone', meaning 'sound' or 'voice'. The 'far off' felt closer when a person physically at the ground would answer, 'Leeds United Club Shop.' A great distance was rendered less so during our brief telephone chat. My body remained firmly planted while my voice and ear travelled (I'd suggest my heart as well, but that's a little too saccharine even for my palate). Marshall McLuhan, no stranger to blunt remarks on the transformative qualities of media technologies, observed, 'When we are on the phone, we don't just disappear down a hole, *Alice in Wonderland* style – we are there and they are here.' This sentiment of a shared location is to my liking despite veering on the side of the fantastic, or at least eccentric. The long-distance telephone call helped adjoin the distance. I was in earshot of the ground, my ear transported to the short reach of another's voice.

In those days, which appear as ancient history today, those calls were my only contact directly with the club. I know that sounds absurd in a world now composed of chats, comments, call-ins, texts, and tweets. Back then, I had neither a kindred spirit like Knausgård nor an Ekelund to share my heartfelt thoughts about Leeds United. I had only the anonymous shop worker, probably annoyed by the frequency of my phone calls, as I crouched alone in my rabbit hole with the cherished cadence of a ringtone.

9

Sunshiny day

ON ANY given week I can enjoy all manner of live football match coverage in the US: the Bundesliga, La Liga, and Liga MX on ESPN+ or Univision USA, Telemundo Deportes, and FOX Sports 2; Serie A on Paramount+ or fuboTV; Argentina's Primera División on Paramount+ (which appears to be the sole provider); Portugal's Primera Liga, France's Ligue 1, and the Eredivisie on DAZN; the Premier League on Peacock and fuboTV; the COPA Libertadores on Fanatiz USA and beIN Sports; Scottish Premiership matches on Paramount+ or via specific club channels (e.g. Rangers TV). This randomly selected week does not account for other national leagues or lower divisions. Other weeks feature World Cup qualifiers, the Copa del Rey, and Africa Cup of Nations or the UEFA Champions League and CONCACAF Champions League fixtures streaming across Paramount+, fuboTV, and Fox Sports 2. A fan of football is spoiled for choice. The world is one big football stream. Swim at your own risk.

Today's reality would have been unimaginable in the late 1980s, when I started to follow Leeds United in earnest. Or, perhaps more fittingly, when I *tried* to do so. I certainly wasn't alone. Even coverage of live matches in England at the start of the 1985/86 season suffered because of agreements among the main terrestrial networks, the BBC and ITV. Once the disputes were resolved, only a set number of matches per season were shown in their entirety, while *Match of the Day* proved the most reliable sources for goals. The role of television in reshaping football, particularly the ascent of BSkyB, is chronicled well by Joshua Robinson and Jonathan Clegg in their book *The Club*. Missing from their rich account is what those of us on the other side of the pond endured to catch the slightest glimpse of our beloved clubs. To make matters worse for me, Leeds weren't part of the First Division until 1990/91, which meant television was damn near impossible.

At about the same time, something changed. The Orlando-based Sunshine Network launched in Florida in 1988 to provide regional coverage, via cable subscription, of the state's sports franchises (new teams like the Orlando Magic and Tampa Bay Lightning, for instance) as well as telecast of college sports. In 1990 the network began to air a highlights show blandly called *English Soccer.* Sunday evenings around 6pm or 7pm became the magic hour, just in time for Leeds' return to the top flight.

I recall the names of teams being displayed on screen (for example, Luton Town v Coventry City) with a voiceover providing few details, mainly the final result of a match, a fixture date, and a league table review. The show, like *Match of the Day*, was based around extended highlights of 'big matches' mixed with shorter segments covering the remaining week's fixtures, typically goals scored or a sending off. This was the only place in my region where I could watch Leeds other than the off-chance of a local pub featuring a match.

Each Sunday, I would pray that we'd be the extended feature, that the announcer would say that Leeds would be the main match of the week. When we were selected for coverage, I'd watch the likes of David Batty, Gary Speed, Gary McAllister, and Gordon Strachan dominate in midfield, players who I only read about, heard about at the pub, or studied in football magazines. In that ten-minute time span on Sunday evening – typically stretched out and revisited thanks to my VCR – they moved, running down the wings, throwing themselves into tackles, delivering corners, making assists, or scoring. I watched in earnest, in admiration.

Failing longer match coverage, I would have to settle for a short segment of a couple of minutes. That was it. Like a roll of the dice each week. One hundred sixty-eight hours waiting for mere minutes on a Sunday. Still better than having to imagine who scored and having to guess how when reading a result published in the *Tampa Tribune* that showed Leeds had drawn 2-2 at home to Arsenal on 3 September 1991. Those brief highlights always left me hungry for more, my appetite for Leeds

United malnourished. Please, Sunshine Network, I want some more.

These were desperate times during the 1991/92 season, when we would win the league and those minutes felt even more monumental, more essential for me to feel involved. This time slot on Sunday evening was where I expressed my loyalty, week in and week out. A permanent fixture. Adding up all the airtime of Leeds in action on *English Football*, it probably fell short of a full 90 minutes. The title-winning season, for me, stuck in the Sunshine State, stuck in front of a television watching the Sunshine Network, left a grey cloud over head. My memory of that season is only a highlight reel. I knew it directly only through time scattered on a Sunday evening watching alone.

For today's supporter, this scarcity must resound like a bleak tale from the dark ages of football; a meagre diet of televised clips in stark contrast to the hearty coverage that the Premier League would soon offer thanks to Sky Sports and lucrative contracts to bring matches to the world's markets. I still find it unbelievable that, when Leeds were in the EFL Championship, I could watch a season's worth of full matches via LUTV or other subscription services. Such coverage certainly attests to the enormous global appeal of football, English football in particular. My memory today is much more vivid, full, bursting at the seams with live streaming, matches and highlights quickly available on YouTube, and fan footage captured on smartphones shared across social media. When not home to watch, I touch my Peacock app on my iPhone (following from the sidelines during my son's football tournaments, which always seem to conflict with a kick-off time). Football is ubiquitous. My precious minutes converted into full days, weeks, months even. No match missed. 'Gone are the dark clouds that had me blind.'

10

Subbuteo, Gatwick Airport

PACKAGING IS more than preservation, protection, storage, and transportation. A container presents information, courtesy of the profession of packaging design. It serves as both a three-dimensional surface for marketing and a physical means for distribution and retail display. A great deal of thought, time, money, and innovation shape every type of package we experience. Enticement is a vital aim. We are drawn closer to handle the package, perchance to purchase its contents and bring the whole lot home to live with us for a short or long stint. Or perhaps, like a candy bar wrapper, we can't wait, rip it open, devour its contents, and (hopefully) discard the wrapper's remains in a rubbish bin. Despite the careful engineering of a package and its ability to stoke our desire, more often than not, the box, wrapper, carton, clamshell, blister pack, bottle, can, tin, or tube is disposed of, cast off, its contents mattering more.

Even so, I find myself in complete agreement with Thomas Hine when he writes that packages are 'an inescapable part of modern life'. He reminds us, in *The Total Package*, that a package is omnipresent, though often ignored or invisible; that our waking moments are inundated with them; and that they easily 'slip beneath conscious notice', despite huge efforts to ensure the opposite effect. I've spent a large chunk of my academic career arguing that the container, i.e. packaging, matters just as much, perhaps in certain cases more so, than its content. I typically write about packaging for video games, whether boxes for software titles for the Atari VCS or cabinets for coin-operated video game machines. Maybe it's the graphic design, colour palette, type, illustration, or physical form that piques my attention. Maybe it's where such products were experienced in the 1970s and 1980s that compels me to want to learn more about the graphic and industrial designers responsible. I'm still trying to process this persistent attraction.

Leeds United is not beyond my penchant for packaging. My centenary badge remains in its handsome blue case, with the club crest and the years '1919–2019' embossed upon its outer cardstock surface. My feelings towards the club's videocassette cases are plain to see in these pages. Most football-related objects – scarves, hats, T-shirts, hoodies, track tops, flags, or strips – don't require boxes. Books on football are an exception, packaged in their requisite covers. The long out-of-print *The Footballer's Companion*, published in 1962, is a particularly precious object of mine with its Lawrence Toynbee cover. Another exception is the box for my Subbuteo set.

The box itself eventually disappeared sometime in the 2000s; only its contents remain to this day. Its arrival into my life was another matter. I purchased my Subbuteo set in 1992 during my first trip to England. At that time, I could not travel north to Leeds and stayed in London, flogging copies of my street punk fanzine, *Welcome to the Real World*, at shops like the Merc and the adjacent Sherry's. I was privileged to watch the veteran punk band Cock Sparrer rehearse at the Stick of Rock pub in the East End, train down to Margate for a festival featuring Peter and Test Tube Babies and the Anti-Nowhere League, and top off the trip with a reggae gig in north London to watch Judge Dread and Prince Buster on the same bill. In the cool timbre of *The Fast Show's*, 'Jazz Club', 'Nice'.

August 1992 was when Leeds promisingly prepared for the first season of the Premier League with that spectacular win over Liverpool in the Charity Shield, only to get knocked out of Europe by Rangers and finish uncomfortably above the relegation zone in 17th. As the defending champions of England's top flight, the club featured on the box of my Subbuteo set. The set itself contained all the expected equipment: tabletop cloth pitch, two footballs and two goals with netting, two teams kitted out in opposing red and blue tops, two goalkeepers, corner flags, and sets of printed glossy paper instructions. Not content with the generic teams, I purchased a Leeds United home squad. Subbuteo isn't common in the US, though scattered leagues and clubs do exist. I cannot boast of playing the game as a child; my relationship began with my first set in 1992. I was 22, enamoured by little plastic men. And my knowledge of the tabletop game, the actual playing of the game, stemmed from way too many repeated viewings of The Undertones' 'My Perfect Cousin' music video.

The opportunity to purchase my own set was simply too intoxicating to pass up, despite the rather bulky box that stubbornly refused to be enveloped by my travel bag. I missed my return flight to the US. The night out in north London was simply too good. I overslept. Upon my arrival at Gatwick Airport, I had to frantically rebook, as my original cheap-crap charter flight with Caledonian Airways had long departed. As luck would have it, a Virgin Atlantic flight was departing shortly. If I walked briskly, not ran, mind you, I would have arrived at the gate just in time. Easier said than done when travelling with two bulky thick canvas bags with a single, rigid zipper holding each shut. No roller boards. No convenient outer pockets. Neither shoulder nor back straps. Just two blistered hands from lugging the heavy, non-ergonomic lumps through Gatwick.

After a half-dozen exclamations of 'Sorry!' for nearly taking out children at my you-cannot-run-in-this-airport pace, I arrived at the gate. Full flight. 'Sir, those bags will not fit in our overhead compartments. You will have to check them.' Fine with me, but not with the scales. My luggage exceeded the weight allotment for checked bags. Too many Leeds scarves purchased, too many Leeds T-shirts crammed in, too many Leeds books imprinting their shapes into the canvas, too many 7-inch and LP records, one too many pairs of Adidas, too many Fred Perry and Ben Sherman shirts, one Subbuteo set. All of this stuff was carefully packed the night before, wedged in with the personal warning: do not open until home; otherwise, you're fucked.

No matter what configuration I tried, my Subbuteo set faced damage. Well, its packaging did. The flight attendant, growing irritated by my behaviour and need to board the flight's final passenger, urged me to remove the box, trying to convince me that its contents would easily fit into my canvas bag. I refused. What made this Subbuteo set special was the photograph on its packaging: Lee Chapman and Chris Whyte in our new Admiral home kit for the 1992/93 season. The photograph-cum-Subbuteo box cover was taken from the infamous Makita Tournament against Sampdoria, when David Batty seemingly took on the entire Italian side himself, wrecking Roberto Mancini along the way. There was no way that I would discard *this* box. It was adorned by a picture of Leeds United players – how could I? That photograph showcased the prowess of the club, champions of England! It was a souvenir of a return to glory.

Refusing to devalue the box, I agreed to board my first journey on a Virgin Atlantic flight carrying my Subbuteo set under my arm, cover image proudly turned out for all to see. I learned to play Subbuteo on that flight, as the game's instructions were my only reading material.

11

Videocassettes, or lived time

I'M SURE many readers still possess DVDs, tucked away in drawers and storage boxes or perhaps displayed prominently in a media console. Those 'digitally remastered prints' and 'special edition' DVDs certainly weren't cheap in their heyday of the 2000s. The likelihood of any of us recouping a fraction of their original price when selling them to second-hand shops, at yard/car boot sales, or on eBay is remote. How about videocassettes? Unlike DVDs, certain videocassette formats have gained a collectable status. I've seen so-called 'big box' releases from now-defunct US distributors like Continental Video or Wizard Video go for hundreds of dollars on eBay. Many of these are in the British 'video nasties' vein, horror, gore, and exploitation titles like *I Spit On Your Grave* or *Colour Me Blood Red* given a second run during the golden age of the VCR and independent video store.

Upon my bookshelves sits a collection of Leeds United videocassettes. When acquired in the early 1990s, either from the club shop directly or from Virgin Megastores and

74

HMV shops, I incurred the additional cost of having each videocassette converted from the PAL (Phase Alternate Lines) video standard to NTSC (National Television Standards Committee). These standards are recorded on the videocassette. The differences are the frame rates (25fps for PAL, 30fps for NTSC) and power frequency (50Hz for PAL, 60Hz for NTSC). This information must read like an ancient, indecipherable language to young readers.

Here's the importance of standards: without conversion into NTSC, a videocassette purchased in the UK (PAL) would not play in the US. My copy of *BBC Match of the Day: Leeds United*, purchased in 1992 for £13.99 at Soccer Scene in London (price tag remains affixed), required an additional $30 so that I could actually watch it. Worth every penny, of course. But the process of conversion wasn't without hassle, namely the need to find a reliable company and the time it took to complete the process.

I have not watched any of my Leeds videocassettes in over 30 years, though all are converted. When I still had a VCR, I watched them multiple times, degenerating their magnetic tape with innumerable pauses, fast-forwards, and rewinds. The content was the means to access players, interviews, commentary, defeats, and victories that I could not see anywhere else. The official club video, *The 1991–1992 Season: Leeds United the Champions*, along with *Leeds United's Race for the Title 1989/90*, felt more like major arteries than benign plastic containers for reels of magnetic tape. Watching that open-bus victory parade from 1992 on videocassette was as close as I would get to that wondrous moment (the pandemic denying another opportunity years later).

Much of this content I reminisce upon is easily enjoyed on YouTube. *Leeds United's Race For The Title 1989/90* has been uploaded for anyone to watch, as has the entirety of the 1992 Charity Shield against Liverpool, played on 8 August 1992, and the 1972 FA Cup Final between Leeds and Arsenal. Such footage is contained on my videocassettes with the others I've mentioned. With football's past so readily available, why haven't I thrown out the antiquated media? It makes little sense to save videocassettes when I don't even possess the device necessary to play them.

Over the years, the value I've reassigned to these videocassettes has little to do with their capabilities as storage media. I've come to appreciate them as objects with the ability to index my years of support. I purchased them all at the time of their original release. Their obsolete status has become a historical marker of my support. As a physical medium entangled in my life, their continued presence, like that of my bucket hat, is a lively reminder of how my support was once innocently enacted.

I can trace my support back to when the medium of the videocassette was the dominant format for storing a season's worth of highlights or seminal matches in the club's history. My memories of winning the Second Division and soon being crowned champions of the First Division appear to me in the format of a videocassette, save for those few matches I could watch in their entirety when shown at a pub. I recall only what was shown, the angle, replay, near miss, pass, tackle, save, or goal deemed a highlight, not what the supporter watching live witnessed. My memories are framed, edited for television. Sometimes in need of adjusting the tracking control for visibility. The quality of being outmoded, however, dates not just the medium but me. That need to acquire such objects, the effort and costs of transferring them to NTSC, all to feel part of the club in the limited capacity of television spectatorship with the benefit of rewind. Their presence marks not just the passage of time but my lived time as a Leeds United supporter.

The action of playback is much slower now, no degeneration of magnetic tape required. My eyes scan their clamshell cases to mentally (and emotionally) replay Eric Cantona's hat-trick in our 4-3 win over Liverpool in the 1992 Charity Shield. The image of Batty and McAllister holding the Charity Shield aloft on the plastic case's spine is forever imprinted on me. I am surprised that such an obscure surface, one just over an inch in width and easily unseen in everyday life, can prompt an emotional impact. It asks that I remain attentive to those moments. Hold on to them. Revisit them. Be surprised and delighted by their endurance. Enjoy their presence like the exultation one experiences when thumbing through old programmes for matches they attended.

In my case, these videocassettes are as close as I got to a match before moving to Leeds. Since they're mixed in with my assortment of academic books, recognising them by surprise punctures the routine humdrum of sliding a finger along spines to pluck a tome devoted to design history or philosophy. They pierce the dull monotony of everyday life and of life lived at a distance. Their continued presence helps to calm those feelings of remoteness. Offer a semblance of intimacy. To discard them because of their technological obsolescence would be an act of betrayal, abandoning the club and the matches I knew only through this medium. A total memory dump. I'd no more abandon them than stop following Leeds United.

12

Stupid o'clock

I TRULY despise the World Cup these days. As the competition has grown and more money been funnelled into certain national leagues, it increasingly takes on the appearance of the NY International Auto Show, where visitors can preview the following season's models. Set aside the cheap façade of Putin's Russia hosting the event in 2018 or persistent human rights violations involved in constructing stadia in Qatar for 2022. It's the transitory spectators that get under my skin the most. Undeserving of the designation of 'supporter', they are spectators at best. They lack history of the game and knowledge of teams and players. They are annoying, their dalliance suspect. But worst of all, when the World Cup – men's or women's – is held in a distant time zone, it's the sense of accomplishment that this lot feels for waking. They take enormous pride in demonstrating their unflinching, albeit short, presence at the odd early morning kick-off to support their national side. Luckily their presence is temporary.

Now, please, don't get me wrong. I too indulge in watching the World Cup (as well as the European Championship). I support Sweden and long still for a side like the one that made it to the semi-finals at Euro '92 and took third at World Cup 1994. But it's no substitute for league play, for Leeds United. I too am walking into a pub, like the King's Head in Santa Monica, at stupid o'clock to watch matches: a pint and espresso working their early morning alchemy. The difference, though, is that this dawn patrol is neither a provisional affair nor a discrepancy from my routine. What passes as a 'lunchtime' kick-off in England is more 'early breakfast' on the east coast at 7am, or perhaps 'late-night snack' on the west coast, with the sound of the whistle buzzing in the head at 4am. Evening kick-offs, too, present an inconvenience. I've had way too many close calls rushing home, having picked up my son from his school, to watch a Tuesday afternoon – east coast time – match, or the dreaded Friday fixture that conflicts with a departmental meeting (with me streaming online in secret, quietly celebrating with a clenched fist when a goal is scored).

Unlike Eric Simons, who in his intriguing book *The Secret Lives of Sports Fans: The Science of Sports Obsession* describes Arsenal supporters who turn out at an Irish pub in the Bay Area at 4am to watch their beloved Gunners play as verging on the obsessive, I find such punctuality and commitment perfectly normal. Perhaps it's odd for Simons, weaned on US sports like college football, or the warm-weather World Cup spectator who loses a few hours every four years, but for dislocated supporters the world over, it's just life.

US sports are designed for television, stretched out across blocks of time to secure more advertising. I've never watched a baseball game in my life. Can't imagine wading through that length of time. American football never held my attention either: too much waiting around, being shown the same play over and over, with play stoppage and half-time spectacles. Basketball is one of the only sports that can make two minutes feel like an hour. Hockey I respect out of fear of a body check. While I'm sure that many will continue to protest that the video assistant referee is making football more 'American' with play stoppages and officials dissecting plays like butterfly collectors, the game itself really demands attention, even if that means watching with one's head propped on a bar counter in the wee hours.

Americans are bred to expect convenience, and their taste in sport is no exception. The Stanley Cup play-offs wouldn't dream of mid-morning games even though it would be more convenient for the huge support that the NHL receives in Scandinavia. Live games, instead, stretch later in the evening, like NBA games, as part of one's evening television viewing habits. College football dares not overlap with the NFL; each sport has its own day of the weekend.

Following Leeds United, or Arsenal for Simon's book, demonstrates the willingness – if not the expectation, given the global popularity of the sport compared with that of baseball – to accept inconvenience to maintain one's commitment. We simply get on with being held to Greenwich Mean Time and fixture changes from Sky Sports. Most Americans do not follow their teams home and away. The vast size of the US makes such a pursuit formidable, with teams located in nearby regions the exception (e.g. Boston Red Sox v New York Yankees, New York City FC v New York Red Bulls, Boston Bruins v New York Rangers, UCLA v USC, Oakland As v San Francisco Giants). Those days lived in League One found Leeds supporters travelling to Carlisle. If those away fans could endure a long journey to support the club, the least one could do from afar was set an early alarm and roll out of bed to represent.

Why, you might ask, not simply record a match to watch at a much more convenient time? Here's my thought on such a question. Watching the match is only one facet in the practice of support. 'Going to the match' is also part of the ritual. It may take the form of an early morning subway ride to Nevada Smiths to watch Leeds United beat Manchester United at Old Trafford in the third round of the FA Cup on 3 January 2010. Or stumbling out of bed, making coffee, then walking a few steps to queue up Peacock or fuboTV on my Xbox – even for 7am matches on my sofa, I feel inappropriately dressed without trainers. It may be thousands of miles from Beeston steps, but it's still a ritual, with friendly banter conducted via texts. And 'being at the match' isn't always possible, so watching live when shown at stupid o'clock is a way to feel connected and share in the immediacy of live play; to be surrounded by the sound of supporters; to gasp when the ball strikes the crossbar or jump up and down in a frenzy on my beleaguered sofa when the ball hits the back of the net. Being away makes watching live even more vital.

I could go on about this ordinary ritual, detail more of its rational impulses, but I must stop. You see, it's almost 3pm on Tuesday, 15 December 2021. We are minutes from kicking off against Manchester City.

13

'Emotion captured' playing *FIFA*

MOTION CAPTURE allows game developers to augment the movements of real-life players. Motion capture suits donned by players enable machine learning algorithms to simulate actual performance and physical behaviours. EA Sports has long touted its ability to deliver not just licensed clubs and realistic animation, but the 'feel' of football, as in the *FIFA 2015* slogan 'Feel the Game'. The tagline promoted the game's 'emotional intelligence', which introduced a range of emotional reactions from the 22 players on the pitch to gameplay. This technical innovation, now common to the globally popular series, sought not only to simulate in-game emotion – frustration from a near miss, celebration from scoring a goal – but to convey that emotional experience to players of the video game.

I don't require an algorithm to experience emotional involvement when playing *FIFA*. I've long worn my own personal emotion capture suit, cultivated an emotional attitude towards playing as Leeds United. *FIFA* and

Leeds, the city and club, are intimately entwined. I first played *FIFA International Soccer* on a PC at my student residence in Headingley in 1994. And I've stayed true to the game since, playing across different platforms and different parts of the world.

Moving from Leeds to San Diego at the century's end – the rush of a high point for the club followed by an even faster downward spiral – my *FIFA* world became much more meaningful. I frequently wrapped it around me like a weighted blanket. The club finished third in 1999/2000 season. Fourth the next. I played *FIFA* daily for hours. Life consisted of finishing that pesky dissertation, watching Sky Sports at 4pm PT, being a regular at the pub for Leeds matches, playing in goal for a San Diego County soccer team, and living in *FIFA* – sometimes until 6am! My starting 11: Nigel Martyn between the sticks, protected by Danny Mills, Lucas Radebe, Jonathan Woodgate and Ian Harte, with Lee Bowyer, David Batty, Eirik Bakke, and Harry Kewell commanding the midfield with Mark Viduka and Alan Smith, ever threatening, in attack.

At the millennium, *FIFA* provided consolation to cope with having left Leeds. My nostalgia wasn't for a bygone era of gaming but for a lost home now over 5,000 miles away. Emotions, the American philosopher John Dewey details, are experiences of the world aimed at things in our environments. An emotional experience always has an object; an emotion that we experience is 'about' or directed 'towards' something. The club possesses an emotional quality for me. Through *FIFA* – the environment of an interactive game – I can access feelings of joy, delight, happiness, frustration, disappointment, sadness. Experiencing *FIFA* through play, I can express my sense of self as a Leeds United supporter. I can 'be Leeds' through daily play. I don't play to escape; I play to remain, to shorten the distance.

The games themselves allow for return visits. I reconnect with previous squads when inserting games into my PS2 and PS3. My memory is external, encoded on an optical disc, protected by a jewel case. I retrieve it periodically to relive, replay, rejoice. From time to time I power up older systems to revisit previous squads, seasons, and cup finals embedded on Sony memory cards and executable via outdated software. I can remind myself through encounters with older *FIFA* titles how near we were to the 2000 UEFA Cup Final and 2001 Champions League Final (we went out in the semis to Galatasaray and Valencia in successive years). A game saved is a life remembered, a past replayed.

Considering my manner of engagement with *FIFA*, it ought not to come as much of a surprise that the point of my play is not to master complex skill moves, acquire the most highly rated players, or play competitively online. I prefer to maintain the current squad, allowing only the most modest strengthening for a successful season, which since 2004/05 has meant promotion back to the Premier League. In certain periods I would start a new season in career mode (my preferred mode of play) by signing a player I always wanted to see run out in a Leeds shirt: Henrik Larsson. I convinced him to swap Barcelona for Leeds in the Championship. In the case of Alan Smith being sold to Manchester United upon relegation, I would immediately bring him home in *FIFA 05*. During the four years spent in League One, I found myself holding on to only a select group of players (Jonny Howson, Jermaine Beckford, Lucciano Becchio, Robert Snodgrass, Fabian Delph, and Max Gradel) when slugging it out for promotion in *FIFA 07, 08, 09,* and *10*. In the dark ages of the Cellino era, 2014–2017, I maintained a core group of players I deemed important for promotion potential (Kalvin Phillips, Lewis Cook, Alex Mowatt, Joel Byram, Chris Wood, Lewie Coyle, Pontus Jansson, and Pablo Hernández).

It pains me to sell players as I try to maintain a semblance of the actual squad playing on the grassy pitch, across an ocean, on my pixelated pitch. I also find myself purchasing players on the transfer market radar of the actual club. For instance, during the January transfer window of 2020, Aberdeen's Sam Cosgrove was purportedly being watched by the club. I studied videos of his goals on YouTube and even watched Aberdeen matches in the Scottish Premier League to decide for myself whether he would fit the squad – as well as mine in *FIFA*. I ended up signing him in *FIFA 20*. Happy with the additions to the squad beginning life in the Premier League, I only made minor additions to mine in *FIFA 21*: I signed left-winger Ryan Kent from Rangers, and Rodrigo

De Paul, an attacking midfielder from Udinese, two players long-linked to Leeds. In *FIFA 22*, I strengthened my midfield options with the signings of Lewis O'Brien from Huddersfield Town and the Sweden international Jens Cajuste, who plays for FC Midtjylland. I also brought in a new name, a young striker, Jordan Larsson – yes, Henrik's son. My current starting 11: Ilan Meslier (GK), Stuart Dallas (LB), Pascal Struijk (CB), Diego Llorente (CB), Luke Ayling (RB), Jack Harrison (LW), Kalvin Phillips (CDM), Jens Cajuste (CM), Raphinha (RW), Rodrigo (CAM), Patrick Bamford (ST). Substitutes: Jordan Larsson, Daniel James, Jamie Shackleton, Lewis O'Brien, Joe Gelhardt, Crysencio Summerville.

Selecting the team and maintaining the actual squad generates a feeling of connection. I tend to lose interest in playing if I'm successful over several seasons in career mode and players retire or if I'm pressured to sign new players or bring through members of the youth squad because of club obligations and my ranking as a manager. I've been sacked for not complying, opting for early retirement over managing a national side, because club football remains more meaningful.

Over my decades of play I've come to associate following Leeds United with *FIFA*. The game is an interactive environment within which I endeavour, borrowing the tagline from *FIFA 2015*, to not only 'Feel the Game' but 'Feel Leeds'. It's where I wish to 'Own Every Moment' – the tagline from *FIFA 17*. Another tagline from *FIFA 97*, uncanny for its ability to punctuate my feelings so well, sums up my relationship best, 'Emotion Captured'. Not the motion capture of players, but the capture of my own emotion within this environment of affective connectivity. I don't play to win; I play to feel.

14

Santa Monica Farmers' Market, a Wednesday in 2008

FOOTBALL CULTURE is no stranger to tattoos. A footballer without a complete sleeve, or at least an assortment of images covering their thighs, arms, and neck, seems out of sorts, strange, a throwback to another era steeped in Brylcreem. Supporters share this penchant for inked armour.

It's nearly a daily occurrence to see Leeds United supporters sporting a picture of a new or first tattoo on the numerous Facebook groups that I frequent. Club crests, portraits of players and managers, signage for Elland Road, slogans, important dates in the club's history, Adidas trainers in blue and yellow, tabloid headlines, and Yorkshire roses are ubiquitous. A quick Facebook search for 'Leeds United tattoos' displays a page devoted to showcasing supporters' work. Over 2,000 people follow the page. I suspect that the same fanfare abounds for other clubs.

I've never counted my tattoos. That question of 'how many' crops up frequently when my students spy a piece peeking out around my collar or shirt sleeve. My first tattoo was done in 1994 at Funhouse Tattoos in Barnsley. I started on my back – not advisable. My pieces range from music- and game-related imagery to comics, toys, and pop art illustrations. I also boast a sizeable number of Leeds tattoos. It's a cluttered and confusing canvas to say the least. I am not prone to sentimentalising my pieces or over-investing them with meaning. I've long been a fan of The Jam, so I have a tattoo. Same goes for Jimmy Cliff's *The Harder They Come*, and for *A Clockwork Orange*. This also holds true for the 7-inch cover of Orange Juice's 'Rip It Up', Italian illustrator Guido Crepax's surrealist/psychedelic character Valentina, and Pedro Bell's drawings of George Clinton flying the banner 'One Nation Under A Groove'. The latter image adorns my right quad with the Leeds coat of arms on the left, its Latin motto *Pro Rege et Lege* replaced with ALAW (All Leeds Aren't We).

I have not yet reached the higher state of Nick Hornby's character, Rob Fleming, in *High Fidelity*. I still believe that what we like matters most, the stuff used to shape our identity to the world. It's impossible for me to divorce my likes from myself. What I am like is an embodiment of my likes. Skin is yet another expressive medium, a carrier of visual messages authoring the self. The recipients are both myself as I wish to be transmitted and others in proximity to the inscribed surface.

That message found its receiver at the Santa Monica Farmers' Market on 23 July 2008. Since 2004 I had lived between Santa Monica and the UK. My partner was based in California while I worked at the University of the West of England in Bristol. I collected a great deal of frequent flyer miles commuting between LAX and Heathrow! Between academic positions, I found myself once again in Santa Monica, living with my partner before we relocated to New York (2008–2016). I was to start a new academic position at Stony Brook University that autumn. My days in July were fairly carefree. I'd go to the Santa Monica YMCA in the mornings and then either ride my bicycle down to the beach to surf or return home to write. Each Wednesday and Saturday, portions of the Santa Monica Promenade hosted a splendid farmers' market. I'd reserve my Wednesday mornings to browse the market to buy fresh fruit and veg for the week.

Something unexpected occurred one such Wednesday. Having finished my workout at the YMCA, I walked to the market in a sleeveless Adidas sports top. Normally, a morning on the coast can be chilly due to the marine layer. On this Wednesday it had burnt off early, so it was warm. The market itself could be crowded with serious shoppers stocking up on pistachios from Santa Barbara, ancient breads, fresh juice, local cheeses, pastries, or whatever vegetables were currently in season, as well as tourists curious about the rich bounty of foods enjoyed by the locals.

Halfway through the market, I heard an unknown voice. 'Is that a Subbuteo player on your arm?' Caught off guard, blinded by the sun, I looked around the crowded street scene to register the owner of the question. More than other places in the world, I find that people strike up conversations with me about my tattoos in California. Usually it's no more than a 'that's cool' or 'amazing work'. Or, in astonishment, 'Oh my god, you have a *Powerpuff Girls* tattoo!' This man was pointing at my upper left arm, where I have a Subbuteo tattoo. The image was lifted from The Undertones' 'My Perfect Cousin' 7-inch picture sleeve. I had the player modified. His kit consisted of a yellow top, white shorts, and yellow socks (an all-white strip is a tattoo's worst nightmare).

I answered, 'Yes, it is,' followed by 'not a lot of people recognise it.' Thinking that this would be just another brief conversation about a tattoo and quickly learning that my inquisitor was English, and with him hearing that I was not, I suspected the inevitable, 'Why do you have Subbuteo tattoo?' or a moment of nostalgia from this stranger who would share his childhood memories by performing calculated flicks in the air at a farmers' market. I quickly proffered that the Subbuteo figure was in a Leeds United strip. That simple line, uttered to offer more commentary on a tattoo to one showing interest, launched a friendship now well into its second decade.

Hearing my comment sparked a change in my soon-to-be friend's face, shifting from pleasant small talk to percipience. He stepped back. His eyes grew large. 'Leeds United? I support Leeds United,' he declared. We entered into a bubble of rapid-fire exchanges, causing a traffic jam for those in search of their weekly bags of spinach or heirloom tomatoes. It turns out that he, Ian Kimbrey, had supported the club since the late 1960s. He cited watching Leeds beat the Hungarian side Ferencváros in the 1967/68 Inter-Cities Fairs Cup Final as the definitive moment. Ian told me that I was coming down to his place in Venice for a traditional English fry-up. Did I have a choice?

His email message to confirm his address was titled 'Marching On Together'. Over breakfast, we talked all things Leeds, bewailing the loss to Watford in the Championship play-off final in 2006 and trying to make sense of life in the third tier of English football, yet another open wound still smarting. Ian showed me his scrapbook from the glory years under Don Revie, including his program for the Fairs Cup Final second leg at Elland Road in 1971 (his ticket stub states a 50p price for a place on the terraces). He even let me use his Leeds mug for tea while we flipped through other programs and player cards. Despite differences in age, occupation (he was an assignment and sales manager at a photo agency when we first met, now a beekeeper for the City of Santa Monica), upbringing (west London, for Ian), and place of residence, we shared in the activity of support for Leeds United.

I've added to my collection of Leeds tattoos considerably since the one spied by Ian at the farmers' market. None have had such a lasting effect as the Subbuteo figure that established a meaningful friendship in that fortunate instance; a flash of recognition, a relationship shared, a mutual identity expressed. Had I worn shirt sleeves, these lines would not exist. I'd probably be writing about avocados instead.

Fourteen years later we are still going strong, like an ageing couple retelling the story of when they met to the bemusement of their wives. We try to meet up once a year, usually by my family and I heading west to stay with Ian and his wife Joanne in their beautiful home in Venice. Ian still serves fry-ups; our red-eye flights are usually greeted with the aroma along with mugs of tea. We text feverishly during each Leeds United match. And we gossip over the summer about new signings, as supporters do. One day, we hope to watch a match together at Elland Road – he won a little money betting on the promotion season, so he's treating us to the Bremner Suite.

15

Leeds spotting

LEEDS SPOTTING. A time-honoured enthusiast endeavour for supporters. It doesn't require a platform, knowledge of train stations, or memorisation of timetables. A camera may or may not be involved. The customary anorak is unlikely, though what one wears is vital. It's a practice I've experienced in too many cities to record accurately, so accept instead a representative sample. NYC: shopping at Lacoste on Madison Ave in autumn 2012. A stranger's gaze cuts across a table of neatly folded jumpers and crowds of shoppers prospecting items on sale to pick out the enamel smiley badge pinned to my lapel. I felt his gaze. It followed me as I filtered through the new autumn line of polos. He bore no distinguishing marks to clue me into his intentions. Had we met before? Was he from the neighbourhood, simply noticing a person he didn't know by name but lived in the same building? I'd never seen him before. Maybe he was shop security and I fell into the category of suspicious-looking people? We made eye contact as he moved towards me.

'Is that a Leeds United badge you're wearing?' he asked in a Yorkshire accent. 'Yes!' in my nondescript American accent that people typically mistake as Canadian. The smiles started. The knowing looks began. 'I'm Leeds too,' he proudly announced. I would soon be asked the inevitable question, 'So how did you come to support Leeds?'

The spotted run the gambit from expats now residing in the US to holiday makers from the UK as well as other parts of Europe. I've exchanged Leeds stories with grey-haired Revie-era supporters as well as the love generation of *El Loco*, Marcelo Bielsa. I've sat in pubs with supporters during Howard Wilkinson's revolution while staring suspiciously at the newcomers donning Nike gear at the millennium's end and went mental with NYC Leeds supporters when Jermaine Beckford scored *that* goal. When spying a T-shirt, top, or scarf, I make a beeline – a club crest beacons guiding me to a safe harbour, doubling as a flare, sent out in the hope of contact, emotional rescue from isolation.

Once spotted, 'Are you, Leeds?' 'Do you support the real United?' A salute to the tune of 'Leeds, Leeds, Leeds' blares. All utterances verbally interpolate passers-by, coordinating our identities in this social moment of address. We are positioned, hailed, named and identified as Leeds. Strangers speak, share stories. We see ourselves in one another, discuss recent matters on the pitch, add to speculation over a new signing, test one another's knowledge of the club, or collectively sigh in misery during the Bates and Cellino eras, now thankfully passed.

It's hard to imagine anything else – apart from a band T-shirt of a certain vintage, perhaps – that could induce the exhilaration, camaraderie, elation of finding another Leeds supporter. Think about it: how often do you stand on a street corner or in an airport lounge with a total stranger, talking for ages? Maybe, as tends to happen, go for a drink? Exchange details? Even plan to meet up again? Friend one another on Facebook? Embrace? Take pictures with one another's family? Such moments intoxicate. I'm exoticised for my support. Proof of the club's global base. A rare specimen photographed as evidence. For me, I'm reminded that no matter where I live, I'm not alone. For a person from Wakefield on holiday with his wife in NYC, the club is indeed global when we talk Leeds in a Lacoste shop to the annoyance of commissioned shop assistants. Something as minute as an enamel badge brings strangers together. A football club becomes a common bond; the world feels smaller.

Living outside of a major metropolitan area these days makes encounters like this one more precious. Each trip to a city brings the prospect of happening upon a Chicago White, New York White, or member of the Los Angeles supporters club.

It also compels me to never travel without badges, a scarf, or some type of signifier to hand in the hope that the visible codes will be read, addressed. Sure, social media allows fans to communicate, share comments, and banter, but the ability to speak face-to-face with a fellow supporter isn't all that common, especially when isolated in a small Midwest town. I need proximity, the physical encounter with my other.

Perhaps I misspoke earlier. Maybe Leeds spotting does share a similar virtue with railway enthusiasts. Like me, they are obsessive types. They collect sightings of rolling stock. Recording their findings in a notebook. I try to sight Leeds supporters. Record those sightings in this short book.

16

The Damned United

TOM HOOPER'S October 2009 adaptation of David Peace's novel, *The Damned United*, enjoyed a limited release in the US. The biopic of Brian Clough's 44-day calamitous tenure as manager of Leeds United played in select cities. New York was one of them. I saw the movie upon its release at a cinema near the Lincoln Centre on the Upper West Side. Peace's novel received its fair share of criticism: the Clough family objected to the book's depiction of their beloved patriarch – they went so far as to boycott the film – while former Irish international and Leeds midfielder, Johnny Giles, took legal action against the book's publisher for defamation. In the same year of the film's release, Phil Rostron gave voice to ex-Leeds players who abided that tempestuous period in 1974 with *We Are The Damned United: The Real Story of Brian Clough at Leeds United*.

In the US, the movie made few ripples. I'd wager that many in attendance were there to watch the performance as Clough by Michael Sheen, an actor known to US audiences for his portrayal of Tony Blaire in *The Queen* and David Frost in *Frost/Nixon* (nominated for Best Picture at the 81st Academy Awards in 2009). The correct pronunciation of the surname 'Clough' baffled fluent speakers of American English. The subject of an English football team in the 1970s, especially one not playing in the Premier League or based in London, was perhaps too foreign, too obscure for the palette of a general audience, hence the limited release. Locally in New York that year, it didn't help matters much when the review for the movie in the *New York Times* led with the tepid title, 'A Soccer Coach Divides and Doesn't Conquer'. I recall reading the review on its publication date to find that Leeds were actually based in the Midlands! Select readers must have complained, as a correction was issued a few days after publication.

What fascinated me about the release of the film in the US wasn't easily spying a contemporary Elland Road in a number of the movie's scenes, arguing about the merits of Peace's writing (I much prefer his Red Riding Quartet and his gallant *GB84*), questioning the casting of Stephen Graham ('Tommy' from *Snatch*) as Billy Bremner, or the rather harsh treatment of Don Revie's legacy at the movie's end. The movie's content matters little to me except for its ability to draw in supporters. 'Going to the movies' became a strange home match.

I lived in Queens, Forest Hills to be exact, and the distance to the Upper West Side was a lengthy subway journey made longer by the pervasive signal failures outer-borough trains were prone to. I'd anticipated the evening since the release date was announced. I'd read Peace's novel before it was available in the US, and I'd followed the fallout from its publication in the UK with intrigue. My wife and I went opening weekend. 'Dinner and a movie', as the date cliché goes, didn't quite capture the event. This was dinner and a movie about Leeds United! A rarity. Drinks would certainly follow, a tradition for us as we discussed what we'd just watched.

It was a chilly and wet autumn evening. I donned the necessary gear for a brisk night out in the city, a pair of Adidas trainers (my pair of Beckenbauers felt blasphemous given the occasion), parka, and Leeds United woolly hat. Oddly, I found myself deliberating heavily on which scarf to bring. I had my reasons. Tradition won. I tied my Leeds yellow-blue-white home bar scarf around my neck. We were off.

I was buzzing when we exited the subway station at 66th Street. That strange, urgent pace experienced walking to a football ground influenced my stride, to the pleas of 'slow down' from my wife. My pace is always quick, was more so this particular evening. In my turn at the window to pay for tickets, I made a hastened slip-up, 'Two for Leeds United,' to the confusion of the employee. Error corrected, tickets in hand, we passed through the vestibule-cum-turnstile.

We arrived early, a bad habit of mine. My first action was to lay out my scarf across the head and shoulder rest of my seat, like a banner hung in the stands for a home match. To my surprise, complete rapture, I was not alone in this action. Other cinema-goers – Leeds supporters – had arrived early at the 'ground' as well, their scarves also spread long across their seat backs. No Nottingham Forest scarves upset our provisional mosaic. All were Leeds. Or at least the majority of the 20 to 30 people in attendance were that night. If I were a sociologist, I might have camped out during the film's theatrical run to interview the supporters who turned out for each screening. Instead, I just revelled in my passion that evening with other like-minded people enacting the same football supporter ritual as I, with cinema seats replacing the stands.

To the uninitiated entering the theatre to watch another one of Sheen's biographical portrayals of a British public figure, the scene was surely confusing to say the least – reminiscent of the set from David Baddiel and Frank Skinner's *Fantasy Football League* television show from the 1990s. Scarves pulled across theatre seats are hardly common on the Upper West Side, let alone across US cinemas. We took the end that evening, proudly showing support, allegiance for Leeds United, even at a cinema! Strangers bound by mutual affiliation in a caliginous interior gave one another the Leeds salute, thumbs up, and knowing glances before and after the match – I mean, film.

Judging from the state of many of the scarves, those in attendance had been supporting for years. Many appeared vintage, obtained in previous decades, removed that evening from trunks, closets, and drawers for the special occasion. We turned up. 'Leeds take more', the mantra for away fixtures, was proven true at an Upper West Side cinema. Fans of the club are certainly no stranger to other sporting venues – consider the support for boxer Josh Warrington – but a cinema, at least in my experience (which is limited, of course), isn't the run of the mill location for football supporters to congregate.

Goosebumps and neck hairs stood upright as we feasted on historic footage of goals and crushing tackles from the Revie era set to the original tune of 'Leeds, Leeds, Leeds (Marching on Together)' as the movie opened. We cheered collectively at Norman Hunter's defensive prowess and Billy Bremner's heartfelt celebrations. We even moaned collectively, and a few whistles and jeers were heard when Sheen/Clough told the squad to 'chuck all your medals'. Boos resounded when the movie ended by deeming Revie a failure with England, depicting a demoralised and haggard-looking ex-manager, alone, with the tagline 'leaving him in the soccer wilderness'. Bowie's 'Queen Bitch' played in the background to laud the eventual newfound European glory Clough experienced with Forest. 'It could've been me' ends with a pensive profile close-up of the actual Brian Clough accompanied by the text, 'Brian Clough remains the greatest manager the England team never had.' Contrary to Bowie's lyrics, my weekend was not at an all-time low. I exited the cinema. Leeds United scarves illumined the darkness. Strutting proudly away. You betcha. Oh yeah.

17

Remember, remember
the third of January

JERMAINE BECKFORD'S goal against Manchester United in the FA Cup third round in 2010 is legendary. The perfect cup fairytale: League One team bests Premier League giants. The Theatre of Dreams turned nightmare. Multimillionaires crestfallen by wage packets. Upstart manager taking the Knight of the Realm. The gulf in class, club status, turned on its head. A beguiling, old-school long ball shocked the reigning champion's defensive high line.

They finish second in the top flight that season. We'd finish second in the third tier. Over 40 teams separated 'us' from 'them'. They go into Europe the following season; we'd enter the EFL Championship to finish seventh, just a few points off the final play-off place.

Nine thousand travelling Leeds United supporters witnessed Beckford's goal that Sunday. The rest of us were jumping, jostling, singing, shouting, hugging in front of television screens the world over. I watched at Nevada Smith's in NYC that morning. The pub was dominated by Leeds, each supporter quietly creeping in, on their own or in small groups, to become united in voice as the match pressed on. Photos were taken afterwards. Numbers exchanged. Some supporters, over from the UK on holiday, others local, and accustomed to east coast kick-off times. The moment stretched out, replayed in conversation, retold round after round. Morning passed into a great day. Becks's goal lives on.

I won't bemoan having to watch matches in a pub. We play the hand dealt, occasionally cheating. For supporters like me, 'going to the match' was a subway journey on a balmy January morning to emotionally cross the Atlantic. The experience of watching in a pub can never be a substitute for attendance at a ground. Impossible.

I am currently without a local pub in Bloomington, Indiana. I watch with my family, text with friends during matches.

Sad, but alas, my current reality. When living in NYC, watering holes like Nevada Smith's (now permanently closed) and Smithfield Hall injected the cultural lifeblood of matches, though, given our league status during the period of 2008 to 2016 when I lived in NYC, not always Leeds matches. Champions League games at Smithfield Hall provided a schizophrenic experience, and probably still do, when the early rounds of the competition were divided up across the pub's different large plasma screen televisions.

I would join my Swedish friends to pull for the Allsvenskan side Malmö FF, perpetual underdogs against all competition in the league. If I had a second team, it would be the Blue Ones. The three or four of us had our regular corner table with a printout taped to the bottom of the television announcing 'Malmö FF v Juventus' or 'PSG v Malmö FF'. I even took my son out of nursery school early to attend these midweek matches to help make up the numbers, and to have him drink in the atmosphere (only apple juice) at an early age. I have a photo of him eating an apple on the E Train and waving a Malmö flag to bemused onlookers.

The scene is memorable and missed, achingly. I never watched Leeds at Smithfield Hall, as our return to the Premier League occurred after I departed NYC, not to mention during a pandemic, when public gatherings were forbidden. I'd turn up in fair-weather form to watch matches with friends who supported other clubs with sizeable followings (e.g. the NYC Hammers). Still, I romanticise the scene. I'm not alone in doing so. George Orwell played a trick on his readers with a thick description of his local pub, Moon Under Water. The chicanery didn't reside in his prose, but in the absence of a real pub. His account, a sleight of hand, pure fiction. The qualities exalted, those of plush Victorian ambiance, ample interior space, no crowding, local regulars, quietude, open fires, a garden, cheap meals and savoury snacks, draught stout, china mugs, and motherly barmaids, are fabrications, alive only on the broadsheet page. A few London pubs possess some of these qualities, but not all, he laments, with the idyllic portrait of a perfect pub forever missing its finishing touches.

Orwell's short piece, published in the *Evening Standard* in 1946, sparks a reverie when I ask what this scene would look like for me. For starters, interior decor would consist of Leeds scarves, flags, pennants, retired replica tops, team photos, and autographed player pictures. Not even the ceiling would be spared, as I love to see scarves hung overhead like polychromatic rafters. Its exterior would be outfitted in a particular colour palette, instantly recognisable from afar, with a large Manchester United doormat to help keep the place clean and tidy. I'd want a name for the initiated: The Lowfields? Geldred End? The Rose and Cheese Wedge? Chip butties and mushy peas on the menu. Tetley's on tap. Bottle openers that play 'Marching On Together' (received one with my centenary gold membership). Coffee and tea served in Yorkshire Pirlo mugs. A Burley Banksy mural. Emma Jones pulling pints. The Athletic's Phil Hay running a trivia night. Micky P. Kerr performing nightly.

The task of imagining such a pub always fails; I come up empty-handed. Where would it be located? In Bloomington, to serve a clientele of three – wife, kid, me? Like Orwell, I should be glad to hear of its existence, but fear I'm left wanting. The action of concocting such a place reminds that I am far from Leeds, far from pubs like Smithfield Hall or Legends, also in NYC, where supporters' groups help manage the distance. In their place, the only banners unfurled are my own, placed austerely over a sofa.

Aside from the win over Manchester United at Old Trafford, when in League One, what made Becks's goal so memorable, so revelatory, to me was that although few in numbers that early morning, we were part of a much grander chorus; singing the same song, in tune in our expression of the moment across the world. The pub played no small part in such revelry, even if imperfect, for it was the supporting stage for those too far to set foot in the stands.

18

If you really love me buy me a (Leeds United) shirt

FOR THOSE not already familiar with the chapter's title, the words belong to Chris Sievey and The Freshies' single from 1982. Neck size 14, blue and red check, long-sleeve, button-down collar is the way to win Sievey's heart. No stranger to delightfully catchy lyrics and tales of prosaic love, Sievey previously confessed his admiration for a certain girl on the Manchester Virgin Megastore checkout desk. 'She sells records,' he sings, 'and that's special.' Buying T-shirts with Leeds United images printed upon them is special too.

'Special' takes on a few meanings.

A shirt is distinguished from others when gifted by a loved one, Sievey's girlfriend, who 'doesn't have to do the million-dollar bit' or 'the bombshell bit to a T', only has to buy him a shirt. My wife, too, who has purchased her share of Leeds United shirts for me, wins my heart with each (a Leeds bathrobe for all of those stupid-o'clock matches being particularly sincere). The use of 'special' in this context points to a distinct quality of the shirt as an emblem of love, friendship. The giver and object given connote the unusual quality we refer to as 'special'.

A shirt can also be held in a certain esteem, 'special', as it is distinguishable from others, a sign of difference. Both apply to my Leeds shirts, though the latter meaning is more of my interest here. A few taps on my keyboard followed by a PayPal transaction and I could easily acquire my bounty from the club shop or supporter-oriented online shops such as the excellent Old School Leeds Co., Forever Leeds, or Punk Football. Alternatively, I might transact at marketplaces like Etsy, eBay, Redbubble, or TeePublic or acquire vintage replica tops and kits from the likes of Classic Football Shirts, Vintage Football Shirts, Retro Football Kits, and the most well-known, Toffs. Even Amazon sells Leeds United T-shirts! But where would I buy a Leeds T-shirt in the US in the 1980s, or even in the 1990s?

I had only a handful of options back then. Mail order from the official club shop was the easiest, though pricey and inconvenient, option. Trips to the UK proved the most direct and abundant source for shirts. When in London in August 1992, street vendors lining Oxford Street were mix-blend goldmines. When I visited Leeds for the first time in 1993 I stocked up on T-shirts at a makeshift club shop at Elland Road as the new superstore was under construction (common in that era of club shop upgrades to the appellation of 'super'). I seem to recall needing two carrier bags, as I purchased around a dozen T-shirts. How I would take them and other things related to the club back home, I didn't know. I wanted one for every day of the week. I never wanted to appear in public without Leeds United blazoned across my chest. It was a uniform for Sgt Wilko's barmy army, a second skin.

These missions were necessary. Sporting goods chains in the US did not stock English football merchandise, unlike now, when the 'so-called' big clubs command shop space in major cities. They couldn't even place special orders at my request. My mail-order sprees also included sending away for T-shirts from ads appearing in the back of *Shoot!* or *Match*. These came with a certain risk. I had to pay the extra costs to acquire an international money order and then cross my fingers that the parcel would actually arrive. Many went missing. Many sellers ripped me off. Little recourse on my end, across the Atlantic.

Another risk concerned quality, or lack of in most cases. British T-shirts were utter crap in the late 1980s, early 1990s. After the costs and long wait for arrival, just one wash would see them completely deformed! The necks lost all integrity: loosened, drooping, stretched almost across my shoulders. The short sleeves became shorter, creeping up to my shoulders. The body looked ballooned, with no shape, floppy, a garment better suited to accommodate an eight-month pregnancy. These, like my highly prized Dennis the Menace and Gnasher T-shirt with the pair wearing Leeds United colours, became converted into sleepwear for my girlfriend or were worn only over a hoodie as was fashionable in hardcore circles at the time. I'd go so far as to cut out the screen print from a distorted T-shirt and tack it on my wall as a poster in an attempt to justify the costs.

The T-shirts craved the most weren't those officially released by the club but the unofficial ones sold by vendors outside the ground. The white ones with screen prints, many of poor quality and easily faded after only a few washings, were unavailable anywhere else. Like Chris Sievey's record-collecting frustration, proclaimed superbly in the song title 'I Can't Get Bouncing Babies by the Teardrop Explodes', those particular T-shirts were beyond my reach. They could be had only by locals at the ground, purchased from a table before or after a match. That's why these particular shirts were so special to me. They signalled a special relationship. They were designed for the occasion of a match and for those in attendance. Not for me, far away. Had I even found a way to purchase them, I'd end up paying more in postage, as they were cheaply priced. Those shitty, deformed ones that I begrudgingly wore, feeling stupid with how I looked as their bottom seams coiled up my waist, were as close as I could get.

The cheap ones outside the ground were superior in my estimation. Not in terms of their quality – I'd eventually have access in the mid-1990s when living in Leeds and can attest to their tracing paper thinness – but for the ability to go beyond the official club releases and tap into supporter vernacular and slogans, display specific player names or likenesses, and best of all, lambast rivals. These shirts possessed an insider status, held an esteem inaccessible to me. Like a record collector's various pressings – bootlegs, test-pressings, or coloured vinyl, needed to feel complete or show admiration for an artist, band, label, or genre – these shitty T-shirts conjured desire for the unobtainable. Lamenting his inability to track down a copy of the Teardrop Explodes record, Sievey paints the frustrating scene with his collection sprawled 'cross the floor from the window wall to the door'. Surrounded by these cherished objects, Sievey declares, 'I'm closer to you,' the anonymous and ever-pervasive 'you' of a pop song. He strikes a familiar chord in the way that a love song can illume one's feelings in a simple, charming lyric.

19

Leeds United at 45rpm

IT IS impossible for me to remember a time in my life when vinyl records were not present. As a kid growing up in the 1970s, I bought 45s and LPs. That practice intensified in the 1980s. My teenager identity was meticulously manicured for public consumption just like the record sleeves I imitated. At the University of Leeds in the 1990s, my financial situation forced me to sell off a large chunk of my record collection to purchase a laptop computer (never got over that). That sale took place 'pre-eBay'. A photocopied list sent to friends in Washington DC, New York, Chicago, and Tampa was the medium. Given the stupid sums being paid for punk, hardcore, oi!, and mod revival records today, I would have quadrupled the amount I made in 1996, which wasn't small, given the richness of the collection. The mid-life chapter I'm writing on my record collecting now takes the form of a record label, Crossbar Records, that I started with a long-time friend and owner of Tattoo Paradise in Washington, Matt Knopp, in 2020.

I have two shelves reserved for books on record collecting and the social importance of music in general. No biographies of Dexys Midnight Runners, Paul Weller, or Ian Dury rest upon those select shelves. Books on musical genres like punk, power pop, glam, and bubblegum, along with histories of labels, lay elsewhere too. Those two shelves help me allay the unquenchable thirst to watch a closing bid on eBay at 1am, map cities based on their independent record shops, strain my back lugging vinyl in my carry-on bags, and squander money on outrageous international postage.

Books with titles like *Why Vinyl Matters*, *Vinyl Junkies*, *Dust & Grooves*, *Vinyl Countdown*, and *Do Not Sell At Any Price* peer from the two shelves. They teach lessons on obsession, schooling me on the sensual pleasures of record collecting: how the needle returning to the groove is a form of reanimation in every play; that the act of listening involves the ears, eyes, and hands; and that our collections are ourselves. My tutors also instruct on the labour involved in collecting: the parlance of the 'wants list', heroic tales of 'the find', embarrassed admissions of prices paid coupled with care, categorising, curating, cleaning, crate digging, filthy fingertips, and Saturday shopping trips. For some, like Graham Sharpe in his *Vinyl Countdown*, an entire book can be devoted to chronicling his trips to record shops the world over. Or, on a slightly different journey, readers could be asked to follow Eric Spitznagel, who in his book *Old Records Never Die* tells of his auspicious attempts to find the *exact* records that he sold earlier in his life. Let me stress this for clarity – Spitznagel doesn't repurchase records he once sold but seeks the actual ones that he owned.

The long appeal of vinyl for me is its tangibility. I lack the fine-tuned ear of the audiophile. I make no claims that vinyl is superior to CD or streaming. That it sounds warmer than the coldness of a CD. It certainly isn't a handy medium. A sizeable collection – not the boutique collection of the 180-gram, Johnny-come-lately enthusiast – takes up space: my living room is a listening room. Secret searches for more storage units are my insomniac porn. I dig the object, even its inconvenience. I like to see storage boxes full. I like to see records displayed in shop windows and anticipate the arrival of an order when 'what's inside' the package is easily detectable by the shape of the mailer, I even like to see their covers greeting me in my 'wants list' on eBay. The record, close to hand, makes the band feel more tangible. Liner notes, lyrics, photo collage inserts, catalogues, fold-out posters, the sleeve's artwork, design, typeface, and record size – all provide the warmth that my ear cannot detect in speaker output. To listen is to look. What the eye sees, the ear hears, the hand covets.

During the First Division title winning season I purchased a 7-inch record from the club shop, 'Leeds, Leeds, Leeds (Marching on Together)'. The song was originally recorded in 1972 by members of Revie's famous side and remixed in 1992, given a more contemporary vibe in the spirit of The Farm's *Spartacus*. I also recall match commentary of a rare David Batty goal laid down on the remix as well. I no longer have the record. I have other Leeds United 45s. In fact, I have the original 1972 pressing, where 'Leeds, Leeds, Leeds' appeared as the B-side on the FA Cup Final single on the Chapter One record label. This record was sometimes spun during soul and reggae nights in New York, when other DJs would open their sets with West Ham United's 'Bubbles' anthem. I couldn't be shown up; I needed to represent.

The 1992 remix is sometimes available on discogs.com, a mecca for record collectors where we can easily share our wants lists as well as satisfy our needs from reputable sources. Currently there is one for sale at £99 plus £15 postage. That's around $150. Bargain. I suspect that with the publication of the recent *Football Disco!*, a visual history of football record sleeves, that prices for these types of records will continue to inflate. The sleeve is yellow with the ball and rose crest on the front cover. The story of the original 1972 version written by Les Reed (known for the Tom Jones smash hits 'It's Not Unusual' and 'Delilah') appears on the back side. The B-side centre label is a ball and rose crest. I always loved that touch. That little bit extra to watch as the record did its revolutions. The Kaiser Chiefs added a similar touch, with their limited vinyl edition of *Duck* appearing in the tri-split colours of yellow, white, and blue. It's a beauty!

As I said, I no longer have my 1992 edition. It was sold in the great scorched-earth sale of 1996. I have a photograph of it. My wife (then girlfriend) knew I missed my record collection when I moved to Leeds. Too big to import, I used to joke. She sent me a photo of a few of my crates and placed the 'Marching On Together' 7-inch at the front of one box. That picture now documents my ownership. I cannot place that record upon my turntable to reminiscence in what probably sounds dated – or perhaps retro – given the fussy state of the music industry.

I am without what Evan Eisenberg refers to as a 'sculpted block of time' when he writes of a record's relation to the past in *The Recording Angel*, another book in that two-shelf collection. These blocks serve as a form of 'modular interior design' for Eisenberg; the collector-cum-architect 'proceeds to pave his day with them'. I understand this action as insulation, a protective carapace.

'Marching On Together' is available in numerous formats, from ring tones to compilations of fan chants on Spotify. What I've lost is a temporal anchor – a specific iteration, the version reissued to mark the historic occasion of being champions. I don't yearn to hear the song but to reunite with the specific record that I once owned. That specific record's status as once possessed by me – or possessing me – has expired. Its hope of return, nil. I cannot make that specific record come to life anymore. And that's why it cannot be replaced by an expensive copy on discogs.com: to do so would be to acquire somebody else's block of time, not the one I experienced through and with that record. The 7-inch possessed power over me. Its production in the first place was to mark an occasion. My acquisition was to join in that occasion, to hold it in my hands, listen to its message of togetherness. *That* record allowed me to talk about *that* moment of the title-winning season. It marked having lived through the event. It was my souvenir. Another's record is just an eBay transaction.

20

Fear and loathing at Adidas shops in the US

I WISH to revisit that short line towards the end of *Fever Pitch* that I briefly touched upon in this book's introduction – one that, to this day, continues to resonate for me, most likely beyond Nick Hornby's original intentions. His sense of tireless support is validated when declaring that Arsenal's victory over Liverpool in the 1987 League Cup Final 'belonged to me every bit as much as it belonged to Charlie Nicholas and George Graham'. Why? Hornby proclaims to have put in 'more hours, more years, more decades than them'. This sentiment is markedly different from his relation to previous Arsenal achievements: winning the league title and FA Cup in 1971. Then he calls into question his own 'contribution' to his club's tremendous season, 'But I hadn't contributed to the Double triumph in the same way, unless you counted a dozen or so league games, a school blazer groaning with lapel badges and a bedroom covered in magazine pictures as a contribution. The others, those who'd got hold of final tickets and queued for five hours at Tottenham, they've got more to say about the Double than I.'

It's understandable why Hornby distinguishes the two achievements based upon his personal commitment. The sense of belonging experienced in 1987 is grounded in endurance, persistence, 'being there', following, committing one's time and life devotedly to the club. The 1971 title felt different because of the lack of 'full-time' commitment, underscored by those more committed, willing to queue 'for five hours'. Duration being the key distinction. Hornby's self-observation helps me work through a tough emotional knot: what happens when your club achieves success and those with *fewer* hours, *fewer* years, *fewer* decades can easily purchase a Leeds United top at an Adidas or JD Sports shop in the States?

When Leeds won the Second Division in 1990, and then captured the First Division in 1992, the success went unnoticed in the US except by the faithful following from aboard. I witnessed no kits sporting the Admiral sportswear logo in shops in the US. I purchased mine during my first trip to the UK that summer, while mail order furnished other objects of endearment. It goes without saying that the Premier League changed this situation, with merchandise for select clubs becoming increasingly available at shops dedicated to soccer equipment (not yet across sporting good or brand flagship stores). For example, once a deal with Nike (a US company) was achieved for the 2000/01 season, when we reached the semi-finals of the Champions League, I could acquire a home or away top at my local soccer shop in San Diego. The silver rail where they hung from the ceiling was jam packed. How many Leeds fans are there in San Diego? Who buys these? I never see anyone wearing a Leeds top at the pub? These questions rushed through my mind.

Walk into any Nike flagship today and you'll find the likes of Chelsea, Paris Saint-Germain, Liverpool, Barcelona, and sometimes Tottenham Hotspur, Roma, and Inter Milan. Leeds' return to the Premier League yielded a kit sponsorship deal with Adidas starting in the 2020/21 season. My wife shared a photo of a recent business trip to NYC, when she made a beeline to the JD Sports shop to see if our 2021/22 gear was present. It was. Sales from merchandise and continued global exposure of the Leeds United brand are hallmarks of the club's success, measured in this context by having our kit displayed alongside the likes of Real Madrid, Bayern Munich, and other so-called 'elite' or 'big' clubs.

Here's the rub: where were these sales, display racks, and consumer purchases over the last 16 years before the return to the Premier League? Unlikely that a top boasting Macron (2008–2015), or Kappa (2015–2020) for that matter, would carry much cache with US consumers eager to sport fashionable brands like Adidas, Nike, or Puma. It's far too easy to chalk up recently acquired 'support' for the club to fair-weather fans, those in the US 'picking' a Premier League team to follow. Thinking back to Hornby; it's highly likely that these fans have never queued even for a minute, let alone five hours. But why would they, when merchandise is so easy to come by these days, and one's relation to a club is remote, mediated by televisual streaming services?

With every Manchester City, Liverpool, Chelsea, or Manchester United top that I see across the US, I cannot help but resent – cue old guy posture – how easy supporting an English football club has become. I certainly am not one to judge their affiliation. But I do find myself questioning how long they've supported their chosen club, as well as how much longer they will. It seems to me that their selection is based upon a limited pool of possibility: only those teams deemed 'good' enough to be carried at an Adidas or Nike shop. Their support isn't durational, in Hornby's sense of Arsenal's success 'belonging to him'. It's a much more convenient, market-driven, fickle affair based on branding power rather than club history. Case in point: how many US supporters of Manchester City can name a single player under Joe Royle or Kevin Keegan? I've ceased to strike up such conversations, as it's blindingly obvious that history matters less than the contemporary moment when one's club is regarded as 'elite' – a world away from the stench of piss at Maine Road. 'Where were you when you were shit?' is a meaningless question here. The blood, sweat, tears (loads of them), and maybe even smells are forsaken by the swipe of a credit card. The measure of commitment and belonging is no longer time but purchasing power. The European Super League may have crashed back down to earth (for now), but the promotion and proliferation of merchandise by only select clubs prevails.

On the day of writing this I happened into the big box sporting goods store, Dick's, to find a rack of Arsenal scarves hanging down from their Adidas cardboard tags. Arsenal, and so many other clubs, now belong to the world market, their scarves only a few aisles away from camping gear and fishing poles.

21

We

'DAD, EVERYONE is Leeds like us!' Words of astonishment proclaimed by my son looking out on to The Headrow from the upper deck of a Beeston-bound bus. Deck was going to his first match, on 11 March 2017, at the age of six. At that moment, along with the entire Saturday afternoon, he 'got it'. His stupefaction evidenced something he had not experienced previously, a sense of being part of something bigger than himself, bigger than the both of us.

The brumous bus window provided perspective, temporarily displaying all of those anonymous cum unanimous bodies scuttering around city streets bedecked in Leeds scarves, woolly hats, and tops – a scene neither visible when watching on TV nor captured in the reading of match reports. The jubilation of proximity explained Deck's shock. All of a sudden, Leeds United abounded. The club was no longer something he sensed only at distance – manifest in his scarf with its sew-on patches, his Kappa hoodie, and his badge-laden knit beanie.

Grandiose and abstract across his life, the club was now brought down to earth, spied at street level, in reach. That day he understood himself differently: no longer a solitary 'I' amid the brine of Adidas or Nike flagship shop supporters but part of the collective performance of 'we'.

The 'it' that Deck 'got' on that mild Saturday afternoon – the feeling of 'we-ness' – became the introduction to an ordinary pronoun made to punch well above its weight. The use of 'we' is a football supporter idiom to verbally self-identify with one's club. It's a tiny word with big meaning. 'We' alerts listeners that the speaker intentionally places themselves together with other people, verbal self-admission into a specific group. 'We' distinguishes and attributes a felt sense of togetherness. This particular word is an intangible means of signifying a feeling of belonging. The song isn't 'I am Leeds', devoid of any social cohesion, solidarity, or collective spirit against opposition tucked into the away-end. 'We Are Leeds' verbalises a group ethos, identity, togetherness, community, performed and gesticulated in every flat vowel sung with arms spread wide.

'We' is a common speech act that, in my early years of supporting Leeds, I struggled with because of its denotative property. In the 1980s I still harboured imposter syndrome when I began to identify as a Leeds fan. I was ashamed not of the club's status at the time but of my own. Hard to imagine a 'we' when only 'I' watched Leeds at my local pubs. More telling of my reluctance to embrace 'we' is that I found myself still (and I perhaps remain) caught in the battle between falsity and genuineness carried over from my punk/hardcore days, when being labelled a poseur meant public humiliation, or worse, getting your head kicked in. The 'wrong' T-shirt or record found in your vinyl collection sounded your subcultural funeral pyre. In the 1980s punk was hard: a stick-together, support the scene, brotherhood/sisterhood unity battle cry of defiance locked arm in arm on (and above) the dancefloor. People invested heavily in their local scenes by being a constant presence at each and every gig, supporting local bands, producing fanzines, making do-it-yourself flyers for shows, putting on gigs, and, lest we forget, defending the scene to the sound of broken bottles against outsiders, who generally took the form of bouncers, jocks, frat-boys, rednecks, and cops.

To internalise this mentality when it came to supporting Leeds proved amendable. How dare I utter 'we' when never setting foot at Elland Road, or England for that matter? That had to and did change. 'We' is a pronoun that one has to earn. It must be filled up with meaning and knowledge, a commitment of self, in for the long haul of the many 'ups and downs'. One mustn't use 'we' lightly or tritely. It's far too convenient to balk at the American who, having recently discovered Liverpool or Manchester City via NBC's coverage of the Premier League, overzealously slots 'we' into conversations about 'their' club. I'm not the person to judge who ought or ought not to embellish their personal sense of loyalty (even if only recently tuned in). Emotions shouldn't be policed.

A world apart: the journey of this dislocated supporter.

My view from the Don Revie Stand against Middlesbrough, 19 November 2017.

Deck proudly wearing his Adidas Stockholm outside The Bielsa on matchday.

Bedroom at my student residence in Headingley 1994.

95/96 Membership Card.

My first Leeds United scarf, 1975. A gift that keeps on giving.

Deck wearing our family heirloom going into our relegation battle final day on 22 May 2022.

More than packaging: image of the Subbuteo box cover from the 1992 edition. My particular box was lost in the early 2000s.

Leeds United videocassettes. Obsolete media as historical marker of support.

Priorities: Streaming the Leeds United v. West Bromwich Albion match stealthily during a faculty meeting on 1 March 2019. Fists clenched tightly under the table as we win 4-0.

Playing to feel: screenshot of my starting 11 in EA Sports FIFA 2000.

Movie ticket stub for The Damned United, *17 October 2009.*

Dislocated supporters celebrating outside of Nevada Smiths, NYC after we beat Manchester United in the third round of the FA Cup on 3 January 2010.

Omayra Cruz, my wife, photographed at the JD Sports shop in NYC and sharing her disbelief at how easy it has become to buy Leeds United merchandise in the US.

Deck's first view of Elland Road from Beeston Hill in 2017.

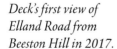

Deck making the journey himself.

Our official papers: Father and son US passports modified to reflect our true nationality.

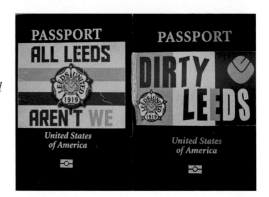

Deck leaving his mark in Malibu, California, November 2021.

Deck's handywork on the London Underground.

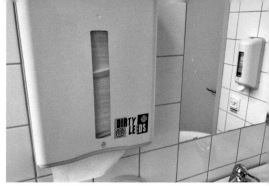

Dirty Leeds at the University of Göteborg

Wrapping myself in warmth: interior decoration in my university office.

Leeds United

🛍 View Shop   👍 Liked   🔍   ···

FIFA 20 Decides! · 9   See All

With football coming to a temporary halt, Leeds United are giving fans the chance to enjoy that matchday feeling! Kicking off at the same time as originally planned, we're letting FIFA 20 decide the result of the remaining Championship games, whilst giving fans a platform to chat with each other, cheer on their team, and hopefully celebrate a few goals!

Continue Watching

SEASON 1 EPISODE 1
FIFA 20 Decides! Cardiff City vs Leeds United
😄 Anyone else bored? How about we let #FIFA20 decide today's result?
37 weeks ago · 187.5K Views

 3.3K

Season 1 ▼

FIFA 20 Decides!: The club's attempt to support its fans during fixtures suspension in spring 2020.

Yorkshire Evening Post, *Monday, 20 July 2020 finally read in March 2022 due to the pandemic.*

Selfie from the stands: Our return to Elland Road in March 2022 after a two-year hiatus due to the coronavirus pandemic.

Deck standing beneath a giant.

Are one's feelings fake, fabricated, a poor facsimile, or illegitimate – a bad cover version? If so, what then is a 'real', bona fide feeling? Is 'we' reserved only for certain, select supporters? Not much of a 'we' then.

I want an inclusive 'we', not the romanticised gatekeeper of my subcultural past seizing upon a different object. I want my son's use of 'we' to feel right for him, with nothing to prove – to anyone – but his enduring love (a father can only hope) for Leeds United. That day on the bus in March 2017 moved him, and I don't just mean to Elland Road. He still remarks on its meaning. We both tear up a little when we reflect on that special bus journey. Deck saw himself, perhaps for the first time in his life, as a Leeds supporter.

22

Beeston Hill redux, 2017

FOR MY son's first match at Elland Road, I insisted that we take a bus from Leeds city centre to Beeston. A more direct route from our hotel via Holbeck meant a two-mile walk. I feared that he might tire from the journey (or more to the point, my back wouldn't hold up from carrying him). Besides, I told him that walking to the ground from Beeston Hill is magical, that his first encounter of Elland Road would retrace my 'first steps' back in 1993. He wasn't convinced that a hill possessed such a quality.

Exiting the bus at a fair distance from the ground guaranteed a decent walk. I pointed out Holbeck Cemetery, sharing the views that it offered for Tony Harrison and, later, for me – explaining why occupying this dual perspective continued to prove so meaningful to me ... and hopefully to him. I thought of Harrison's poem, *v.*, as my son spied graffiti. I even thought to myself what the word 'united' might mean to him. A one-club city? Our relationship, father and son, going to our first match together? Our little collective 'we' joining one much larger as the hours sped to 3pm? He reached for my hand as we walked closer towards the steps. We smiled at one another in anticipation. Me imagining a father who could have shown me the way, Deck having one who knew the way.

I explained: I want you to experience the closing of distance upon your first visit. We travelled so far for this exact moment. I didn't want to prolong it but only to pause, to enjoy the flutter of anticipation, feel the closeness advancing with each step, the hill's treasure soon revealed. The banal action of traipsing down a hill in West Yorkshire became profound. Its discovery in 1993, a happy accident turned tradition that I passed along to my son, a boy born into a Leeds United family visiting his adopted native soil for the first time. No other route desirable. This tradition is remarkable in its ordinariness, the privilege and pleasure of being able to tread where so many local supporters do each matchday.

The East Stand revealed itself. Our pace quickened. We turned down a side street. The end of housing, beginning of grass. Our eyes drank in Elland Road. Deck perched himself upon a railing, elevating himself above discarded cans, rocks, and assorted rubbish. Seeking an even grander view. Standing taller to measure himself against the fortress. Too much for the eyes. Too much for the heart. I was already choked up. Eyelids failing to hold back tears. Not only walking to the ground but overcome with emotion along the way.

We stood together closely. It's OK to weep at beauty. My hands on his shoulders. A loving – and knowing – embrace. My question of 'are you ready?' breaking the brief silence. I pointed out the long steps to Deck. 'See those?' I asked. 'I want you to make the journey yourself,' I insisted. I brought him this far. I wanted him to carry on alone, to have an intimate, quiet moment, to reflect on all of the matches that he'd watched on a computer screen, all of the stories about the club that I had shared, all of the player footage he'd watched on YouTube, all of the scarves that decorated his bedroom, all of the club kits he'd played in and would outgrow, all of the *FIFA* matches he'd played as Leeds, all of the patches his mum sewed on his first scarf knotted snuggly around his neck on that brisk March day. I wanted him to perpend, as a six-year-old could, what this experience might mean to him as his stride shortened the distance. He was here.

I followed behind, but not too close, so that Deck could move at his own pace, in his own time, perceive the experience from his view. Wonder. Dream. Elland Road pulling him forward, towards his arrival, exciting his senses. The photo I share captures his descent: the tiny figure marching on but not alone, soon to be joined by thousands. Until other bodies formed the matchday scurry, Deck had this sombre moment with the concrete paving the way towards his destination. He waited for me at the bottom of those long steps. A proud look on his face. We were here.

We drew with QPR. Deck stood the entire match high up in the Revie Stand, scarf proudly tied around his wrist. Deck sang his heart out, no hesitation whatsoever, his voice growing raspier as full time grew near. Most words to the repertoire of Leeds songs known by him though he confused the word 'bastard' with 'bucket' each time the QPR keeper took a goal kick. 'You shit bucket' bellowed weirdly. Even the steward stood at the back with us laughed. We left Elland Road with no 'first goal' witnessed. Still, disappointment was nowhere in sight.

The steps lining Beeston Hill felt colder now, even longer somehow, as our ascent was met with gentle mist making all surfaces sheen. This time I walked up the steps with Deck. Hand in hand. We dissected the match. Discussed chances not taken, the flatness of play. Bemoaned the lack of a goal. The exchange felt natural, an ordinary back and forth between two football supporters mulling over a lone point rather than all three. Better than a defeat, I reminded him. When we reached the top of the hill we turned back towards Elland Road as other bodies quickly passed, the mist turning to rain. Deck, his face a shimmering surface, soaked up the view again, not to say farewell but to ask when we were coming back.

23

Passport ready

IN THE US, passport requirements were originally a provisional affair, periodically invoked during periods of war from the American Civil War through World War I. Passports became required with the onset of the US's involvement in World War II, and by 1978 it was illegal to enter or exit the country without one. US passport booklet covers have, over the years, ranged from red and green, with a dark blue hue adopted in the late 20th century.

According to the US Citizenship and Immigration Services, the passport is a document that establishes one's identity as well as legal employment authorisation. It tops a long list of documents that include other forms of identity verification such as US passport cards, permanent resident cards (also known as 'green cards'), foreign passport/ immigrant visas with I-551 stamps allowing the possessor to stay in the country for up to a year, I-766 temporary authorisation documents granting limited employment, I-94 arrival/departure customs documents (those forms one fills out upon arrival in the US), and the state-issued driver's licence (the subject of another chapter). One's personal data is stored on the electronic chip housed on the back cover of the passport (supposedly by the image of the Earth's moon). An image of a microchip on the passport's cover signals that it is biometric – bureaucratic technology for the technocratic state.

Not only does the passport document its holder's national identity, it projects images in accordance with a pictorial narrative of nation. Inside pages are awash with 18th- and 19th-century imagery of landscapes, animals hunted to extinction, loads of different birds, mighty vehicles of the industrial revolution, a clipper ship possibly off the coast of Nantucket, an overall-clad lone farmer with his team of oxen, a group of cowboys wrangling cattle, and only one woman, the Statue of Liberty pushed to the near end of the booklet, with an image of an orbiting satellite suggesting more territories to conquer (our newly formed Space Force at the ready). No people of colour appear in the US passport, bar an indigenous totem pole and an incredibly difficult-to-recognise image of Diamond Head in Hawai'i, its image covered in blue text, sacrificed to administrative information. Is the passport now a pictorial civics lesson or pocket-sized scrapbook of Americana?

Such bucolic scenes appeared in the US passport when George W. Bush was in office, and it's hard not see the two-page spread of Mount Rushmore – more white guys – morphing into the headquarters of Trey Parker and Matt Stone's *Team America*. Fuck yeah! The then secretary of state, Colin Powell, approved this redesign in the flavour of 'merican patriotism when the White House still served 'freedom fries'. Prior to my most recent passport, issued in 2012 and due to expire a few months after writing this chapter, I adorned the back of the booklet with an American flag sticker delivering the message 'we aren't all dicks' underneath.

Upon the passport booklet's midnight blue cover resides the US Department of State seal, an eagle – in an implausible position evoking an amateur tattooist's lack of perspectival drawing skill – clutching an olive branch in one talon with 13 arrows in the other, the number 13 also represented in the field of stars for the country's original states. Supposedly, the eagle's glance on the side of the olive branch signifies the nation's devotion to peace, with defence always at the ready. Or, from another perspective, a trojan bird. This eagle, in such an unnatural posture, must politely cover its crotch with a shield embellished in the colours of the US flag. In the eagle's beak, like a flailing worm for its hungry young, is a banner espousing the Latin, 'E Pluribus Unum', the motto for the US, 'out of many, one'.

Another motto emblazons my US passport. Placed over the silly bird seal, neatly affixed just below the word 'PASSPORT' in all-caps and right above 'United States of America' set in the serif typeface Minion, is a sticker reading 'ALL LEEDS AREN'T WE'. It's carefully placed, seemingly fitting into the existing design. Stephen Coles's *The Anatomy of Type* describes Minion as the most 'vanilla of serif typefaces', one making little visual impact when applied. Cole asserts that its application is best when 'you really don't want anyone to notice your type'. I cannot say the same for my sticker, or the one on my son's passport stating 'DIRTY LEEDS'. I want 'my type' noticed. A sticker in the approximate blue hue of its surrounding surface is a handsome addition, an example of the namesake spelling out one's country of origin: the word 'minion' means to prefer over others as in a preference or, favourite. Seems fitting to state my preference upon such an important document, one granting me entry into other countries, not to mention my own.

Surprisingly it isn't a crime to cover the 'Great Seal' on a US-issued passport. The name of the document, 'PASSPORT', remains visible, as does its country of origin. That gold text does its job of stating the nature of the document. Nothing is damaged, destroyed, removed, or forged. It is only unlawful for another person to use my passport. And the only other regulatory requirement is that its bearer sign the document underneath, you probably guessed, yet another image of an eagle. This one has a very large head and looks a little uncomfortable with its Mona Lisa smile. My unflattering photograph – as we've come to expect in official forms of ID – is awkwardly surrounded by pink and light blue stripes extending from a waving flag. The abbreviation 'USA' sits upon my head like a clumsy halo. 'USA' and 'United States of America' appear five times on the so-called data page, where my digitised photo is affixed into an amber wave of grain. The placement of my sticker offers no interference to this machine-readable zone.

I have travelled for years with my sticker placed over the Great Seal. I expected on its first usage that a US border security officer, tasked with screening passengers entering the country, would refuse my entry, or at least require that I remove the sticker or proffer some nonsense about it being unlawful to deface a US passport. I refaced it, by the way, not defaced it. The routine of having one's passport open for scanning seems to have negated this possibility. When spied by a customs or TSA officer, a look of confusion appears across their faces, nothing more. In the UK, especially when arriving at Manchester Airport, the stickers are always a source of amusement for customs officials. We usually engage in friendly banter or discuss a latest result. I respond to the inevitable 'why are you visiting the UK' with two words, 'Leeds United.' Again, warm spirited laughs are shared. My son chimes in, 'We are going to Elland Road,' when he receives the same question, or when he's asked, 'Are you really Dirty Leeds?'

I've customised my passport to reflect my chosen identity, not the one incurred by birth. A football club affixed over an eagle. A different seal of affiliation espoused. Club over country. Literally. *E Pluribus Unum* revised to read *Omnes Ledes Non Sumus*, an approximation at best. A different motto to embrace, embody. A similar sentiment of camaraderie, unity, belonging, 'we-ness' not indicative of citizenship. One that travels. Made official upon entry. Showing it – and myself – to the world, proudly.

24

REAL ID

MEREDITH CASTILE'S wonderful little book *Driver's License* explores the history, social values, and meanings of the US driver's licence, as well as the administrative role the document plays for national security and state regulation.

On the book's opening page, she describes this legal instrument as the 'talismanic pass to life': an official means to prove one's age in order to operate a motor vehicle; purchase alcohol and cigarettes; travel domestically; gain entrance into clubs, bars, concerts, and some movies; buy a gun; join a gym; open a bank account; gain employment; vote; and even get a tattoo, among many, many other services and institutions that require one to flash their driver's licence to prove their identity. She also notes the pure joy of acquiring or faking a driver's licence, a rite of passage for many underage teens before barcodes, holograms, microprinting, UV images, laser perforation, and magnetic strips denied such circumventive (and illegal) pleasure.

With a measure passed by Congress in 2005 known as the REAL ID Act, originally set to come into effect in 2021 but delayed to 2023 because of the pandemic, the Department of Homeland Security will require a REAL ID-compliant driver's licence or a state enhanced license to legally fly within the US. A compliant driver's licence possesses a 'star' in the upper right corner of the card. This feature alerts the Transportation Security Administration (TSA) that one's driver's licence is a certified REAL ID.

I refuse to accept my Indiana – or before that, New York, California, or Florida – driver's licence as my 'real ID'. The colour scheme is all wrong. The phrase 'INDIANA USA' appears in red, of all colours! No Leeds United crest appears in microprint, or as a hologram. No images of former players or managers appear. A formula car signals the Indianapolis 500 (an odd image of speed for a driver's licence). It simply does not present my identity to the bouncer allowing me into a bar or match the 'LUFC92' on the licence plate secured to my blue car.

I hide my driver's licence in my wallet. It is nestled behind my current 2021/22 gold membership card. Many wallets have transparent plastic 'windows' where one is expected to house their driver's licence, given its frequent and required usage in the US. It never dawned on me until writing this that for over 20 years I've carried a Paul Smith wallet that does not conform to this design common in the US. My Paul Smith wallets were always purchased at Heathrow duty free when travelling between the US and UK. Plus, they hold currency larger than the US ugly biker tattoo dollar. So, when opening my wallet, one immediately spies my Leeds United membership card: adjusted higher than the other cards it accompanies like a floodlight towering over Elland Road (at a much different scale). The other bits of identity – my driver's licence, university ID, debit and credit cards, medical insurance, and my AARP card, among others – are relegated to insignificance, near invisibility in the tight pockets of my wallet.

Establishing the identity that I want to project on to the world isn't limited to the displacement of my driver's licence. When photographed for official documents like driver's licences, passports, or university identification cards, I always make a point of wearing a Leeds top or having a badge (typically a smiley crest) present. The photograph usually crops any visible markers of self despite my best efforts, bluntly enforcing my 'pass through life' along narrow channels of officialdom. Still, I try where possible, refusing to hide. Upon my Tumi backpack, purchased on sale and used for nearly a decade, I must have looked perplexed when the shop assistant asked if I wanted my initials monogramed on the bag. I responded by saying, 'Why on earth would I want my initials? Use LUFC instead.' Now the look of bewilderment rested upon his face. I am not interested in having my initials project from my back. I want the world, as the backpack accompanies me on international and domestic trips as well as to and from campus, to know the football club that I support, not my name. 'MOT' is the monogram upon another bag. A sign thrown up hoping to catch a knowing eye.

In the physical places where one's identity is shown, inscribed, or positioned for another to observe, you could say that I choose side before self every time. A document like a US state-issued driver's licence is meant to tell someone who you are through data of the most banal variety: legal name, address, gender, height, weight, eye and hair colour, organ donor status, birthdate, and expiration date (the licence, not mine). And of course the dreaded and more often than not unflattering Department of Motor Vehicles headshot. Combined, these data are designed to reflect a 'me' that I rarely recognise when scanning my driver's licence (or when, more likely, somebody else does in the prelude to a speeding ticket). It fails to equate with my version of myself, one that must include vestiges of Leeds United to achieve any approximation of my REAL ID.

I do find pleasure in the small act of supplanting my driver's licence with my current membership card. The state is deemed secondary, tucked away from view. It does not define me. My reordering prevails. In fact, when asked for my ID, I usually jest (or jeer) by flashing my membership card. I know that it will not gain my entrance on a plane or grant passage to a drink. It may not even be regarded as a joke, receiving scorn from a cop or bouncer who holds that 'this is no laughing matter'. And I agree, the club that I support isn't a joke. But still, I persist, demanding to have Leeds United as a direct part of me, ever present as I pass through life. 'Self' and 'side' cannot be separated, and my REAL ID isn't measured in weight, eye colour, birthdate, or an issuing US state.

25

Written in the sand

'MAN U are Scum' unexpectedly greeted passers-by to the University of Leeds one snowy winter day in 1995. A field of brilliant virgin snow adjacent to the Roger Stevens Building bore the declaration, imprinted by an anonymous artist. The large letters were scrupulously marked out, unavoidable to the eye in the Brutalist quarter of campus. The words greeted me early that morning. Their sheer scale delighted, as did the audacity of their author's gesture, a despoiler of a rival's success (Blackburn Rovers would win the league in the 1994/95 season). For a fleeting moment, snowflakes spoke. Strikingly.

This act of gesticulation sticks with me. I am compelled to dig my heel not into supercooled water droplets but into fine rock and mineral particles forming beaches worldwide. Beaches upon which I tread are marked with giant letters forming the inevitable 'LEEDS UNITED'. Like an allied soldier scrawling 'Kilroy Was Here' or a kid from the South Bronx going 'all city' via a tag on a subway train in the 1970s, my mark is meant to display presence but without the use of markers or spray paint. The public surface is sand, rather than walls or buildings. Like a graffiti tag, my work, if it can be described as such, shares a distinct signature, not of an artist but of a club, 'LEEDS UNITED Was Here'.

Or at least, that's how I feel every time I drag my heel across the sand, tagging a beach. It's a peculiar habit. Each letter formed carefully. Lines straight. Capitalised for emphasis. Sometimes followed by a 'Rules OK!' or 'Nuff Said'. No secret, no hidden meaning. Just blunt text. Personal association made public. Affirmation. The message certainly won't remain. I often stay until the incoming tide leaves only a blobby distortion of my work behind before time erases the last trace. Yet, the futile action continues. Staking another beach, at another time, somewhere else. The question for me is always, why? Why such persistence? Aren't sandcastles enough?

With each 'LEEDS UNITED' inscribed upon a beach, I send a rescue signal, hoping that another supporter will respond. No one has so far, but I press on with my heel writing to tempt the curiosity of fellow beach goers. Maybe someone will ask about the activity, enter into a spontaneous conversation about football. That dragging heel also issues a warning: Leeds United are everywhere, even here on your holiday at the beach, accompanying your fishing, beach party, volleyball, or surfing. As beachcombers saunter along, seeking shells, prized sand dollars, or to study sea life braving dry land, they may hit upon my inscription. Read it. Seek its author.

Perchance, pending their temperament, desecrate with walking stick, feet, or hands. Will satellites hovering the Earth relay my message? Is it visible from space?

This sandy surface loosely inscribed points not back to me as its author but to the social communicative ability of the letters and proper noun they form. I've simply arranged a code to be deciphered over an ephemeral duration determined by a tide table. Will onlookers reuse my inscription? Reapply it in their own conversations, 'Someone wrote Leeds United on the beach today.' Will it resonate? Will another understand? Will it reach another Leeds supporter, or a fan of another club who will then adopt my practice of sending messages in the sand? As with a graffiti tag, some will decipher the message while others will decry its presence, denounce it as vandalism, or fail to register it altogether.

The fleeting nature of my inscription compels me to revisit this practice time and time again. From southern to northern California. East and west coasts of Florida. Scarborough, Agadir, Jones. No beach is spared. The text distorted from the tide's frothy advancement, for a few moments at least, leaves only a trace of my message. But what of this trace? The German philosopher, Walter Benjamin, once asserted that 'to live means to leave traces'. He was referring to one's interior dwelling: how we inhabit our home, imbue and accentuate our personal place with memories. The private realm, according to Benjamin at least, is where our traces are most prominent. We leave our impressions on our interiors. Think of the objects that you surround yourself within your home. What clues do they provide the visitor of who you are?

My little harmless act of writing in the sand can never leave a lasting impression. For it will always be fleeting. The tides guarantee that. It is in the act of perennially forming those letters – LEEDS UNITED – that I subscribe to Benjamin's sentiment. The traces I leave exceed my home, exceed me, as they are often left behind as happy finds for others to puzzle. So much of my life has been connected to Leeds United. If to live is to leave a trace, then inscribing a beach is yet another space – place – to imprint one's life. Scoring these letters in the sand helps me feel nearer to the club even when at great distance, like writing one's name, the name of a loved one or friend, or an image of a heart on a foggy window, in undisturbed snow, or through one's own breath on glass that was itself once sand.

26

(Sticker) bombing cities

LIKE THE fleeting beach tag, small, palm-sized stickers invade the peripherals of everyday surfaces. Lamp-posts, bicycle racks, safety railings, buses and trains, building site barricades, trash bins, toilets, public utility signs, and countless other banal public surfaces are trespassed – transgressed – by little printed pieces of paper or vinyl. 'Stickering', 'sticker scene', 'sticker culture', 'post graf', and 'street art' are terms used to account for the practice of adhering 'slap tags' to the above objects. Having grown out of graffiti, punk, and surfing/skateboard cultures in the 1970s and 1980s, stickering too warrants the nomenclature of popular art, a newspaper box or stop sign preferred to the bromidic walls of the white cube. Taken out of its urban environment, the sticker loses its context; its physical location expresses creativity or conflict.

Stickers, in my mind at least, enliven ordinary surfaces with flashes of colour, text, and image. They direct our eyes to surfaces overlooked or only ever glanced at in passing. Working in groups – which is often the case, as a barrage of layered stickers share popular objects turned expressive signage – they embolden a community ethos of coexistence, a place for all, even if crowded. I first began stickering in the 1980s, mainly punk rock stickers consisting of band logos. This was a low-key affair, just an adolescent act of benign vandalism, imposing my musical sensibility in the eyeline of others. The more offensive the sticker (e.g. 'Millions of Dead Cops') the better. Over the years, my preferred arsenal for bombing cityscapes has turned exclusively to Leeds United stickers. These aren't official souvenirs from the club's shop. They are acquired via online mail order. Back in the early 1990s, snail mail ordering delivered my 'Leeds Fans Against Nazis' paper stickers from the fanzine *Marching Altogether*. These were too precious to me to adhere to actual surfaces, so I bootlegged my own via late night trips to my local printing shop.

I never travel without my cadre of adhesive vinyl. Whether stuffed into my wallet, or in a secret pouch in my shoulder bag, I'm always well-armed, sticker bombing the unsuspecting with rectangular missives of 'Dirty Leeds I Predict A Riot', 'Leeds Vile Animals On Tour', 'The Pride of Yorkshire', 'Super Leeds', 'Dirty Leeds Aren't We', and 'Marching on Together'. A jaunt with my son along Sawtelle in Los Angeles offers bicycle racks and lamp-posts to decorate. Peel off the backing. Place it in pocket so as not to litter. Glance around. SMACK. Move on.

Northern California is illuminated as well with Bay Area Rapid Transit (BART); the streets of San Francisco and Palo Alto are gifted generously. An innocuous midday journey on the London Underground's Northern line proffers a fitting juxtaposition that my son (then aged seven) immediately executed: the seating sign posted for the differently abled announcing its reservation for 'people who are disabled, pregnant, or less able to stand' was affixed with 'Warning: This man can seriously damage your health' depicting a photo of Gaetano Berardi headbutting Bristol City's Matty Taylor. The seat was unoccupied at the time, should the reader question my parenting. New York's MTA – especially the E and R subway trains to Queens – enjoyed interior redesign when I still resided in Forest Hills. Streets along the popular football pub, Smithfield Hall in NYC, may still reveal residual traces neatly placed over a Chelsea sticker. Return visits to Leeds begin at Manchester Airport, where the odd remaining payphone box, toilet doors, railings, and the train station are prime targets.

As an academic, I would travel regularly to conferences in the US and Europe prior to the pandemic. No trip to a university, city, or hotel for an annual conference would be complete without stickering. An invitation to speak at Goethe University in Frankfurt, December 2017, provided train stations untouched by my hands as well as many food stalls at the city's festive Christmas market. Talks at Concordia University in Montréal compelled strolls down the beautiful Rue Sherbrooke to observe public art while adding some of my own. Apologies to the Quartier de Musée.

Scandinavia isn't beyond my reach: IT Copenhagen, Malmö University, the University of Gothenburg, and the University of Oslo are well loved. 'Dirty Leeds' slapped on a hand towel dispenser in a toilet at the University of Göteborg felt like too good an opportunity to pass up. Hotel elevators are another favourite interior. Many bodies, ascending or descending, at the Society for Cinema and Media Studies or Society for the History of Technology annual conferences have cast a curious eye at what my hand has left behind.

Each sticker left upon such assorted surfaces is a marker signposting that I – we – have passed through this space. Frankfurt's Ignatz-Bubis-Brücke was the path taken for a day out record shopping. The bridge's steel framework hosted many football stickers slapped down by locals as well as travelling supporters. 'Ultras Frankfurt 1997', depicting an image of a member of the Baseball Furies from *The Warriors*, gets tagged out by 'The Pride of Yorkshire'. Leeds United are back in Europe; at least in the form of stickers. The world's side streets that we slip down are stickered Leeds. Reminders placed in a chosen spot. Public peripheries emblazon white, yellow, and blue. Grounded. Located. Homing signals set. The transient nature of life – just passing through – pauses to quickly alight upon a spot and then move on.

I rarely feel alone during these touristic jaunts. The club is in my pocket, its presence susceptible only to weather, rivals, and cleaners tasked with abluting the surfaces of life. Each sticker is part of a much larger mosaic, like one fan is accompanied by 36,000 at Elland Road multiplied globally like a square in Charles and Ray Eames's *Powers of 10*, demonstrating the magnitude of our belonging, altering our perception of the world.

27

Office scarves

I AM not alone in the decision to adorn my university office with merchandise associated with sport. I spy colleagues doing so frequently with their own collections of Indiana University swag. Collegiate sports have never captured my attention. Even prior to going aboard for my graduate studies, I lacked any enthusiasm for them whatsoever. Perhaps I never enjoyed the proper indoctrination to cultivate any true passion. Or, most likely, have no regard for any sports that require a tailgate party to make them interesting.

In my office, scarves, pendants, flags, tea mugs, and stickers dominate the space. Mugs with broken handles or chips gain new function as pencil holders. I cannot bear the thought of discarding them. I assign them new tasks so that their surfaces continue to communicate their yellow-white-blue messages, surfaces that still impress upon me even if held together by a hastily applied epoxy. Flags add colour to bland walls that reek of institutional insipidity, thoughtless interiors surrounding those whose labour is thought. Building maintenance will surely issue a report on my application to walls and bookcases of stickers with slogans like 'We Are Leeds, Dirty F*CKING Leeds', slogans most likely indecipherable to staff gorging on the Midwest diet of college basketball. Even brushing past my office to the elevator or stairwell, students and colleagues glimpse the battle cry 'Stay Calm and Keep Marching On' on my window, dotted with a smiley crest, another alien symbol in this part of the world. I am alone. Isolated. Landlocked. Fucked.

Upon entry into my office, it is the scarves that elicit the most attention. They crawl down walls with thumbtacks anchoring thinning threads. They stream across books erratically arranged on shelves, covering over their spines with the letters S-U-P-E-R-L-E-E-D-S-U-N-I-T-E-D and an assortment of club crests from years gone by. As the desirable locales of walls and bookshelves become increasingly overpopulated by acrylic-polyacryl-elastane blends, my ceiling receives its own treatment. For the visitor to my office unschooled in the culture of football scarves, this is indeed an odd assemblage: woven fibres designed for personal warmth reborn as static office decoration. Printed words, club crests, or assorted images of a face (e.g. Bielsa) prompt curiosity, questions about a name, likenesses, or even 'what's Leeds United?' or 'what's Pride of Yorkshire?' I've unintentionally curated my own cabinet of Leeds United curiosity.

But for me, the interior designer deftly schooled in the art of matching coloured thumbtacks to tassels who sits at the centre of this sanctum, this abundance of scarves serves the purpose of orientation. They take up residence in my office, a constant presence upon my visual horizon. Their message is not external – they aren't crude territorial, tribal markers – but one directed internally, becoming the walls enclosing me. In their presence, I write, read, check emails, scan the *Yorkshie Evening Post* online, doodle, flip through books, drink coffee, talk to students, hold meetings with colleagues, prepare for class, buy records at discogs.com or eBay, eat, think, daydream, plan travel, stream music, and sometimes even fall asleep from boredom. Mostly I wait, these days for the ability to travel again. To return to Leeds, to be at Elland Road. My scarves are gathered and displayed around me as coverture for a prolonged sadness in the wait to return. They swaddle my longing, for I belong elsewhere.

I endeavour to direct my feelings towards them so they, in return, can evidence, contain, and return it in kind, a happy reminder. My enduring companions, always hanging around with me, direct me beyond themselves. They take me back to their arrival. Many were purchased at Elland Road, or outside the ground via stalls heaped with mounds of screened polyester. They are placeholders pointing back by their presence, pointing back to a happy place.

In gathering scarves over the years, displaying them in my office, they serve not only to orient my feelings to Leeds United but to intentionally restrict a certain view. They block my immediate surroundings: Bloomington,

Indiana, the Midwestern United States, North America. Places that I wish neither to see nor to be. My entire visual horizon is filled with Leeds United. My eyes have no other option but to drink it in. The ordinary, perfunctory space of an uninspiring university office is not spared from my need to envelop myself in Leeds United. The ordinariness becomes all the more crucial. The office is where the daily experience of work and living occurs. It mustn't be exempt from the emotional connections I maintain.

I want Leeds United to be familiar, an inherent part of life. I have to work harder at it, employ conscious practices to skew this worldview to realise another. Transform my daily life, no surface left undisturbed. An office wall? But another opportunity. Surfaces committed to the cause. Pressed to make an impression, intensify sensation. The blunt force of being there. Protruding into my bodily space. A new shelf-life. Abating distance, even if the means for doing so takes the form of materials imbued with happy and hopeful feelings. That is what I wish to see, not my immediate existence but that which cannot be my everyday.

Scarves are necessary materials for cultivating the everyday life that eludes this dislocated supporter. Their fibrous cohesion moves me. I feel closer by their stark presence. Displayed in my office, they provide the warmth I desire.

28

Three for a Fiver

RITA FELSKI'S book *Hooked*, touched on earlier, explains the function and feeling of attachment, the experience of being captivated by, or drawn to, a song, novel, painting, or favourite film. Had I dared such a daunting task of study like the renowned professor of English at the University of Virginia, I would have gone with *Pricked* as my preferred title. I feel that irksome sensation each time I fumble around with a Leeds United enamel badge, trying ever so cautiously and precisely to position it on a denim jacket, parka, suit top lapel, or flat cap, among other articles of clothing. At some point during the dance the inevitable happens. My large hands drop the teensy badge. I pick it up. Bundle my second or third attempt. Then, ouch! Thumb or forefinger redden. Tiny blood droplets percolate through the skin's surface. I'm attached – literally, not just emotionally – to my object of affection with the wee pin dangling from my distended digit. Love hurts.

Why go through the bother? Why pierce pinholes in so many garments? A denim jacket can take the abuse.

They are made for it and look nude without badges nestled securely on front chest pockets or collar. Same goes for a parka. Without badges, it's just an oversized raincoat, an embarrassment to its wearer drowning on the inside. But a suit top is another matter. The risk of ruin inevitable. In my book, the fantasy one at odds with Felski's title and this one, the enamel badge is a magical object, one its wearer imbues with powers of allegiances, significance, and self.

We enact the badge's magical properties when we feel incomplete without the physical presence of its signage. When we dare not wear a jacket without an enamel badge affixed upon a lapel. Or, in my case, when my garments are always already pinhole punctured, hung in the closet with their badges intact, the two disparate items unified – a badge for every occasion, for every day. Because of their diminutive size, these badges require extra care. Otherwise, they are easily misplaced or lost. Despite their ability to pierce surfaces, they can come loose; a butterfly clutch pin can fail, or the badge itself can snag and fly off. We must actively attend to them. They are needy little things.

I've devoted considerable time to these shiny pricks. Their minute size suggests a precious relationship. They need me to not lose them, to ensure that the butterfly clasp or rollable clasp functions properly and that they are stored in a safe manner. I need them to mark identity, offer a physical invitation to onlookers to move closer, look sharper. I need their detail, insignia, to companion my life;

provoke, invite, deter, evoke. Ultimately, I want an enamel badge worn upon a lapel or pocket to connect me with other supporters, to signal camaraderie and togetherness as I transport them through daily life. They entangle me in a football culture public, asserting my presence and identity as a Leeds supporter. Each time a badge inscribed with a smiley crest, 'keep the faith' with a soul fist, a mod target in blue-yellow-white, or the trophy for the 1992 champions season receives recognition, it performs its duty, connecting me quite literally and physically to a club. A large gesture for a tiny thing.

I proudly wore a mix of badges in the 1980s, mostly to broadcast the punk bands that I followed. My first Leeds United enamel badges were acquired in the early 1990s when visiting England. I've purchased a few on eBay, but that practice always leaves me cold. The thing is, I'm seduced by eyeing a fleet of enamel badges pinned into a cork board outside of Elland Road. In the mid-1990s, I'd buy them along the road itself. An older gentleman had a very tall, narrow cork board littered with the little shiny things, each drawing me closer like a signal mirror. So many slogans to choose from, 'We Are Leeds' being a personal favourite. Club crests across time all present in that moment. I'd covet badges with the coat of arms, LUFC in script, the owl, smiley, and of course the beautiful 'rose and ball' crest. Badges were quickly added to a scarf or a collar (otherwise, I'd place them in my jean pockets and forget about them or reach in and receive a piercing). A trip to Elland Road meant a new enamel badge. And on occasion you'd observe a fellow supporter whose cap was weighed down with a heavy assortment of badges to transform the cloth into a helmet. Television cameras seem to love them, unable to resist lingering on a supporter with their scarf ornamented, cotton frayed by so many little holes. It's notable that such supporters appear older, perhaps showing their roots in sew-on patches, or CND peace signs. Or even punk, as we've all aged.

Enamel badges, though, are not reserved for the pensioner. When visiting Elland Road in recent years I still purchase them outside the ground. A vendor offers the 'bargain' of 'Three for a Fiver' just near the Lowfields Road. My son bought a Minions figure in a home kit, a blatant attempt to attract a much younger generation to the blood ritual. My jubilation at seeing so many badges displayed, shining and singing LUFC slogans, remains. I eagerly hand over my fiver, sometimes more, to enlarge the stockpile.

I feel obligated to purchase. This teensiest of acquisitions marks being at Elland Road for me. Each tied to a specific match, a specific visit. Perhaps for the season ticket holder, these physical markers of memory are redundant. Those fivers would certainly add up across the season. For me, the badge acts as a placeholder of sorts to say that I'm here and will return. But the enamel badge is far more than a mere souvenir. It's a companion in life, something that travels with me, is worn close to the heart. It's that little bit of ordinary attendance at Elland

Road that eludes me and that I must surround myself in even at the risk of pain; an intimacy not forgotten but in constant view, an emotional relationship preserved in enamel.

29

The lift at the DoubleTree, Leeds city centre

BOXING DAY 2018; Leeds United 3 Blackburn Rovers 2. Our journey began on the previous day. My son's Christmas morning was hijacked by an afternoon flight out of Orlando in order to make the 3pm kick-off. Once we arrived in Manchester Airport I splurged on an Uber because of the lack of trains running on Boxing Day. As luck would have it, we were able to check into our hotel room early, partially wash away the jetlag, and change for the match. We selected this particular hotel for its convenient access to Leeds station and for its proximity, which allows us to walk to Elland Road. There was also another reason for favouring this particular hotel: the squad stays the night for home fixtures.

I am not one for autographs, and I shy away from requesting a selfie with a player. I'd certainly consider doing so should my son want a picture taken with a player. I suspect that the players just want to be left alone in their private pre-match mental prep. We spied Kemar Roofe sitting quietly in the lobby sinking into his earbuds, a clear 'do not disturb' sign that needed to be respected. I gave a slight 'all right?' nod to Finnish defender Aapo Halme, who didn't quite settle into the squad before moving on to Barnsley in the summer of 2019. Mateusz Klich looked so unassuming in his glasses, just like a hotel guest who stepped out to buy a newspaper and have his first cup of coffee. My son did request a selfie with Pontus Jansson, his favourite player, but the big Swede was nowhere to be found. His consolation prize was a scarf with Jansson pictured in his magic hat.

I suspect part of the reason why I'm reluctant to engage with a player is that awkward feeling of not knowing what to say. When living in Los Angeles, I'd experience 'star sightings' all the time. I nearly knocked Christina Ricci on her ass in a crowded restaurant in Los Feliz, had to endure Jason Swartzman's snarky commentary while watching a film at the New Beverly Cinema, witnessed an angry Gary Coleman walking down Santa Monica Boulevard when on the same day the opposite scale of man in the form of Kareem Abdul-Jabbar walked past me (in hindsight all I could think to say was 'skyhook,' like I shouted when trying his signature move as a kid). Quietly, and slightly scared, I observed an angry Chris Penn tear into an anonymous party on his mobile one morning on the Santa Monica Promenade. Not-so-Nice-Guy-Eddie. I also once shared an elevator with Edward Norton after watching the Spike Lee film *25th Hour*, in which he starred. Talk about breaking the fourth wall! In these cases and more, I never once felt compelled to say anything. Look away, rather than look stupid, was my preferred tactic.

That tactic let me down on Boxing Day. Descending in the hotel's lift – a contradiction, I know – we were on our way to the match. On one of the floors below us the lift stopped. A figure, preoccupied, seemingly talking to himself, busy in the mind, rushed in. It was Marcelo Bielsa, well into his first season as manager and soon to be a club legend. I do not know how much time we shared. He exited precipitously before the lift reached the ground floor. It's like he left something valuable in his room, remembered, and dashed out to retrieve it. In that short duration of time it felt like the stupidest grin that I could make was fixed upon my face. I felt shock, joy, and pure delight, but my face probably said something like 'don't ride with this lunatic, get off on the next floor'. My son Steve McQueened the situation. As Bielsa stepped into the lift, he saw our colours, he knew why we were on that lift, and that we knew who he was. Making eye contact, my son swiftly made the Leeds salute, proudly tapping his chest in honour, respect, and appreciation. Bielsa smiled at him in return. I was still frozen, deranged looking. No smile for that insane-looking person whose jaw had to be scraped off the floor of the lift.

Exiting the lift, I ushered my son to walk quickly around the corner in our excitement. Our jumping and hugging for joy was like a mutual pinch in disbelief. We just shared, albeit for probably ten seconds, a lift with Bielsa. I looked total crap, my face trapped in another temporal dimension trying with no success to form itself. Deck was dead cool with his instinctual gesture of solidarity. One acknowledged with kindness. That chance encounter was our topic of conversation for the walk to the match. We collectively replayed it, and with each retelling I looked worse. Even my son took the piss! We experienced a moment that many supporters of Leeds United witness and share regularly on social media: Bielsa sightings. Bielsa's ordinary qualities and humble demeanour are often celebrated in the form of pictures of him walking along sidewalks to training, pushing a shopping cart through Morrisons in his training gear, and posing with fans in Weatherby where he resided. A coffee at Costa is cause for a tweet.

Our time in the lift on Boxing Day was our moment of Leeds everydayness. Though it was evanescent, we got to experience the delight of a casual, random encounter with Bielsa. A trivial activity turned phenomenal, its fleeting quality sustained by the action of writing, recording those delirious seconds beyond their actual temporality. We were gifted a Leeds story, like those of so many others who post their sightings.

The match on Boxing Day also offered exceptional quality. In the previous match, we beat Aston Villa 3-2, having to come from being down by two to do so. Roofe scored the winner in that match. He would do so again against Blackburn deep into injury time. We sat just outside of the North Stand, towards the bottom of the lower East Stand. Roofe's winning goal, a collective sigh of relief, propelled my son towards the heavens. He'd have reached that destination had his foot not been caught in the folded-down seat that he was standing upon to watch when I threw him in the air in jubilation. He bounced around on the heads and shoulders of other supporters before regaining his footing. Nearby supporters rushed the sidelines. Bodies crashed upon my head. Bodies jumped, clapped, screamed, sang, hugged. Pure joy. Our section and those surrounding Elland Road transformed into a giant scrum to celebrate that crucial win. My son's woolly cap was returned by a fan sat a few seats down from us. His foot bruised and sore from nearly being ripped off his leg, his mother would remind me of my responsibility as a parent when we returned.

He asked why I reacted in such a reckless manner, his wellbeing tossed away in a moment of unbridled joy. I explained: you can't feel like this when watching on TV or a computer. Nothing else but being here feels this way. Elland Road is that one place in my life, hopefully his as well, where we can let our emotional guard down, be completely ruled by our passions, share love and loyalty, put aside our daily responsibilities and expectations, allow ourselves to be unravelled, experience emotions so intensely as to sing and hug strangers and even catapult your only son into the frigid air. He forgave me for the bruise and started to show it off like a scar sustained in battle. Friendly fire. Limping back to our hotel, we resumed our reflection on having shared time with Bielsa in a lift. Sadly, we were brought back down to earth during the following match when Hull City beat us 2-0 at home.

30

Love in the age of a pandemic

THE SCRAPBOOK containing the material traces of my son's trips to Elland Road stops abruptly. It hasn't run out of pages. Its binding remains intact and capable of holding more mementos of our pilgrimages to Leeds. Many pages, though, remain empty, unfilled with photos, tickets, and newspaper clippings I collect from the *Yorkshire Evening Post* when in Leeds for matches. Since November 2019 those vacuous pages, often quietly stared at in the hope of glimpsing some sign of normality's return, have been a miserable reminder of a world struggling with a pandemic.

Their blankness is testimony to absence, to the inability of being in the world beyond one's personal Zoom *cordon sanitaire*. Their lack of use places living on pause, unsure when those pages will once again have new memories to protect and store. The cosmic 'blip' from the *Avengers: Infinity War* movie: Peter Parker's (aka Spider Man) despairing cries of 'I don't wanna go' as his body streaks into dust, ceasing to be, echoes strangely with my plight of not being able to go. Sure, it's not the end of my being, but it still hurts.

My mussed handwriting in the margins of the scrapbook notes that we beat Middlesbrough 4-0 at home on 30 November 2019. That was our last trip for a while. One that was also meaningful on account of receiving the official news that my student loan had been forgiven because of my service at a public institution – fitting to receive this news when in Leeds for football! And, retrospectively, I recorded in the scrapbook that this was the only centennial match we attended due to Covid-19. My son and I had tickets to the Fulham and Luton Town matches in March 2020. We planned to watch Cardiff City away with friends in Headingley during our spring break in Leeds, at Elland Road in particular (for us, tea towels happily replace beach towels). We also prepared to return to Leeds in May, in a solemn pact, to take part in the open-top bus parade through the city centre to join the celebration of being crowned champions. None of this happened, sadly, disappointingly, maddeningly. We intentionally delayed cancelling our flights, living in false hope, until my university announced that travel outside of the US would not be supported. We were even willing, at my best parental discretion, to run the risk of being barred from re-entering the US if it meant the opportunity to attend more matches! That fantasy was short-lived. Two days after we cancelled our trip, EFL matches were suspended. Had we travelled, we'd have had no matches to walk to.

For a period of time it felt like those barren scrapbook pages engulfed the world, with their clear polypropylene protectors shielding all of us from airborne contagions. Our lives flattened out, glued down behind a precautionary membrane. Matches would eventually resume in the eerie conditions predicated aptly by the German *geisterspiel* ('ghost game') without supporters. Soundtracks tried in vain to simulate fan presence while 'cardies' (photo cardboard cut-outs of fans) filled the stands, though they always fell flat in their support, if you ask me.

Leeds United provided life support of sorts in the form of its FIFA 20 Decides!, a watch party on the club's official Facebook page and on Twitter in which the club's remaining fixtures were played on the *FIFA 20* video game. 'With football coming to a temporary halt,' the club announced, 'Leeds United are giving fans the chance to enjoy that matchday feeling! Kicking off at the same time as originally planned, we're letting *FIFA 20* decide the result of the remaining Championship games, while giving fans a platform to chat with each other, cheer on their team, and hopefully celebrate a few goals!'

Live-streamed gameplay for the postponed Cardiff away fixture boasted 600 shares and over 120,000 views before half-time in the video game. Around 300,000 people watched via Facebook, and the match generated over 2,800 comments: a strong testament for a social platform in the absence of matches. In the reality of FIFA 20 Decides! we beat Cardiff City 3-1, whereas at the Cardiff City Stadium we lost 2-0 on 21 June 2020. I turned up at all of the FIFA 20 Decides! matches, as they offered a place to be in the absence of regular fixtures.

We would, regardless of the above result, be crowned champions of the EFL Championship in July. There was no open-top bus victory parade through Leeds city centre. Fans descended on Elland Road to celebrate with the squad locked behind the ground's gates, players singing and clapping in support of fans from the East Stand on the evening of 17 July once promotion back to the Premier League was confirmed. Bodies also amassed in the city's Millennium Square on 20 July: the summer sunshine and sheer jubilation of ending the 16-year hiatus from the top flight of English football proved too potent to maintain social distancing protocols amid a blue-and-yellow-flared street party. For those unable to make the party, barred by an ocean and international travel bans, the scenes of celebration were intoxicating but cut with personal dejection, daily death rates forcing our distance.

I spent those joyous mid-July days glued to social media footage of rapturous supporters. Twitter felt voyeuristic, like peering into a private party. All those videos uploaded to Facebook helped those blipped enjoy a sense of belonging, share in the revelry even if only as spectator. The shared mobile phone footage, shaky, twirling, tussling in the pure, raw excitement of its user offered the imperfect view of frenzied passion, there for all to see, to join in the jerky jubilance. My family, kitted out in Leeds tops and scarves, uploaded a selfie to Twitter.

In fact, I uncharacteristically joined Twitter on 18 July just to feel closer to the club, players, and other supporters. I craved social interaction. I needed to observe, to witness and be witnessed at the event. I longed to physically sense the air sliced by a scarf swiftly spun overhead, or clog my lungs with blue smoke, or embrace strangers in solidarity with the long struggle. I needed to upload that group selfie into that social space as a token, as a desperate means to 'be there', to take some part in the carnival occurring across the blue-and-yellow globe. Friends emailed all day to send their congratulations (as if I personally played some part in the feat).

We streamed BBC Radio Leeds just to hear voices from Leeds, just to embrace the excitement heard in unabashed utterances. I collected screenshots of the trophy presentation on 22 July, little moments frozen in time of the players' joy. And I asked my friends in Headingley to grab copies of the *Yorkshire Evening Post* and store them at their house for our return one day.

Conclusion: Blipped

THOSE BLANK pages of my son's scrapbook have changed. Life restored. Pictures of Deck at Elland Road, our tickets to the Norwich match on 13 March, and an assortment of clippings from the *Yorkshire Evening Post* are all now neatly affixed. The blip in time remains marked by the dates of match tickets: 30 November 2019 to 13 March 2022. Two years and then some, an absence book ended by these small pieces of ephemera turned indications of time ceded – painstakingly endured – during a perduring pandemic. Fuck! Has it really been that long? Yes, agonisingly. Supporters had returned to the stands long before we did. I'm bound by my son's school holidays, and my university schedule. Tickets became unsuspecting attestations, markers of a most painful duration.

Those copies of the *Yorkshire Evening Post* with dates like 29 June 2020 and 20 July 2020 were collected from my friends upon that return trip. Now, two years later, I can slowly thumb through a newspaper with the bold, exulting headline, 'WE ARE CHAMPIONS!' I don't relive but live-for-the-first-time those delayed moments of exuberance captured in local print. There has been no shortage of books documenting and showcasing the title-winning season, so why is a thin 88p newsprint paper so valuable to me? A newspaper, like other forms of ephemera, according to Maurice Rickards (the foremost authority on the medium and the founding chairman of the Ephemera Society in 1975, with a collection fittingly bearing his name at the University of Reading), is one form of the 'minor transient documents of everyday life'. Rickards's elegant definition for cheaply produced paper documents, the lifespan of which is intentionally temporary, speaks to this flimsy, insubstantial form's ability to invoke the past through the topicality of its printed visual and textual messages.

A book like the club's *We Are Leeds* that chronicles the championship-winning season doesn't provide the sensorial experience needed to feel a sense of belonging to that moment in a way that an ageing newspaper can. The 20 July 2020 issue of the *Yorkshire Evening Post* gifts a 16-page 'We Are Going Up' special pull-out section, complete with player profiles, key matches towards promotion, and a review of all of the years – tears and cheers – since exile from the Premier League. Holding this object in March 2022 proffers a strange sensation. Many of the players pictured in celebratory, candid expressions have left the club. Its creased pages document a now-distant period, one of hope for the first season back in the Premier League, read amid a relegation battle in spring 2022 as I write this book's conclusion.

I deeply value this particular edition for its ability to record the title and the city's celebrations, from which I was sequestered. I deeply value the ink smudges glossing my fingertips. I'm thrilled that the ink still smudges after two years, seeping into the arch, loop, and whorl patterns of my identity. It feels eminently personal, like the daily grime of life, as if I purchased the copy myself from a corner shop, perhaps still a little hungover from the weekend's party that summer. The status of the newspaper being a 'daily' plays into the local fantasy that I harbour, in which the routine of its acquisition is not extraordinary. It's a surrogate form of belonging: a friend's hand picked up this newspaper in place of my own. The more I gently caress these wrinkled, thin pages, the more I try to imagine myself there, each touch reaching out across the geographical and temporal expanse. A newspaper imbued with substantial meaning, properties to enliven, restore, renew.

Collecting copies of the *Yorkshire Evening Post* in March 2022 also serves to mark our return to Leeds. I waited over two years to do so. I did not want to run the risk of having them vanish in the postal tides. The return to Leeds required the obligatory visit to Beeston Hill and Holbeck Cemetery. There we stood at the Harrison family marker. I shared the two views of Elland Road, the city and university, with my son. They hold no opposition for me. I've long aligned them. Using one perspective to orient the other. Next, we walked down the steps of Beeston Hill together, side by side, for Deck has made this journey numerous times previously. No need to enforce its symbolism, only to indulge in and appreciate its ordinariness restored, the fortuitous stride of finally being able to make the journey anew.

Along Elland Road, Deck spied an Illan Meslier scarf outside the ground, hung over a fence to entice passers-by. Player likenesses on those digitally printed bootleg scarves never do anyone justice. Quality, though, isn't measured in likeness but location. The 'unofficial' status was yet another marker of closeness for us: we were in reach of the indistinctive vendor's table, back at the club we love so. There in the proximity that made even a bootleg scarf exotic and wonderful. 'Three for a fiver' had become 'two for a fiver', we quickly learned when seeking out the person selling enamel badges. It could have been 'two for a tenner' and we'd have happily paid for these minuscule pricky souvenirs.

We both selected smiley crests in chubby 1970s-era 'Super Leeds' font. Deck opted for the traditional yellow on blue smiley; I chose the less-popular inverted colour arrangement: two sides of the same coin for a father-and-son team. We even purchased a shopper cotton bag for Ian Kimbrey, watching the Norwich match over 5,000 miles away and at the stupid o'clock time of 6am Pacific. The gift was perfect: a market bag, a reminder of where our friendship began so many years ago when he asked the innocuous question, 'Is that a Subbuteo figure tattooed on your arm?'

We rounded out our trip to Leeds with romps around the city, walking hard down The Headrow, Briggate,

Park Row, Albion Street, Boar Lane, Merrion Street, Woodhouse Lane, Great George Street, Holbeck Moor Road, Beeston Road, Noster Terrace, and Elland Road, of course. Our feet grew sore from endless heavy treading across the city. The blunt blows of stone upon our feet grounded us. Blisters, a tender reminder of place.

Remembrance wasn't had only in our soles but in our hearts when snapping a picture of Deck under the Marcelo Bielsa Way sign, or when peering at his Hyde Park corner mural, not that far from my old flat in Headingley. Our return was not just to the ground and city but to a bare bucket (Sisyphus's rock?). On Sunday, 27 February 2022, supporters of Leeds United obtained a new epithet, *Las Viudas de Bielsa* ('Widows of Bielsa'): a designation for fans across the world who had cherished their time spent with this most humble and principled human being. The moniker fits.

On that day, the ensuing week, months after, the phases of grief ran their course. Denial, first. Those horrific results across the month of February, nearly 20 goals conceded in four matches, could be turned around by *El Loco*. We just need injured bodies mended, a shuffling of the current squad and positions, more flexibility in form and style of play, I told myself. Anger followed. Bielsa put too much faith in certain players, needed to abandon the man-on-man defence, and use strikers not wingers up front. The board failed to invest in the squad. In the club's official statement, chairman Andrea Radrizzani described the decision to part ways with Bielsa as one of his 'toughest'. Being an ideologue has its limitations and consequences. A game of rock-paper-scissors played only with a clinched fist. The need to stave off relegation being the ultimate justification, the apologia for the ultimate sacrifice. Early in 2022, we were reminded of just how bleak the situation was with the sobering statistic: we'd won only five matches thus far in the season.

I certainly was not alone in sifting through feelings of grief and regarding Bielsa's time at Elland Road as more than a mere management role but a renewal of the city, a restoration of faith in the club. We had experienced the sackings-merry-go-round in the Massimo Cellino era, from who-the-fuck-is Dave Hockaday to Thomas Christiansen (who as I write currently manages the Panama national team, if that's any testament to his time at Leeds). Between those names are five others, none worth mentioning. Bielsa was different. Not just in the form of winning a title, but by providing comfort and sanguinity to years of disarray and uncertainty. An article on the Marching On Together website expresses this sentiment well, 'He brought us back together. It had become a rarity to see club colours worn in the city outside of a matchday, but Leeds shirts made a return, telecoms boxes were transformed to white, blue, and yellow as murals went up all across town. Bielsa not only restored Leeds United to the Premier League but also our pride.'

A writer for *The Guardian*, James Riach, goes as far as to say that Bielsa's dismissal 'leaves a hole not only in the dugout but also in the heart'. Bielsa's influence in

West Yorkshire – the world further afield – had supporters questioning, Riach continues, 'Why they bother watching football in the first place?' In the spring, supporters shared photos with him across social media. He said his goodbyes for five hours outside Thorpe Arch. Touching tributes abound. He is and will remain well loved at Leeds. He gave us hope when we had little. He taught us to believe again. Dazzled our eyes with his style of football. Won our hearts with his sincerity, humility, idiosyncrasy, and genuine kindness. Valued hard work, integrity, loyalty, faith, and compassion over the spoils of the so-called promised land. He is a philosopher committed to his beliefs, a man of principles. Though Bielsa departed, his presence remains.

The 'Bielsa phenomenon' bridged local supporters and the legions spread across the globe. Fans everywhere poured out their hearts. The city marked itself – murals, street names, Burley Bansky's artwork – in his image. He proved a galvanising figure, one generating togetherness; Leeds fans were widowed with others across the world in France, Chile, and Argentina. Collective grief, and grief collected, shared the world over. Those tears shed once learning of his dismissal weren't shed in isolation. Looking back now with a new manager at the helm, one who provided an indelible result against Norwich upon our return (and again, on the day of our departure away to Wolves!), Bielsa's gift to the city, club, and supporters was to remind us how good it feels to be Leeds no matter where you are.

Epilogue: Marching On Together

THIS BOOK was wrapped up, ready to deliver to the publisher the first week of May 2022. Yet it felt premature to hit 'send' with so much at stake: feelings rollercoastering from the highs of beating Norwich, Wolves, and Watford in March-April to the stomach-wrenching plunge of losing to Manchester City, Arsenal, and Chelsea. It felt like the poor run of form from February had returned with a fierce vengeance for daring to believe that we could stave off relegation.

Red cards.
Old injuries.
New injuries.
Lack of goals.
Leaky defence.
Keeper errors.
Chances not created.
Poor passing.
Possession lost.
Pressing abandoned.

Questionable substitutes.
Set pieces haunting us.
Tactics unclear.

Fingers can be pointed in multiple directions: Bielsa's purported insistence on a 'lean squad' (or refusal of those players being offered), the owner's inability to invest well, the appointment of a new manager (inheritor of a squad lacking confidence, prone to injury, appointed after a transfer window and with no experience even in English football, let alone the Premier League). Speculation and accusation abounds, as does frustration, disappointment and despondency. We are forced to dine at the table that has been set regardless of our appetite.

I found myself seeking comfort in two places. The first, hardly surprising, is a playlist of Leeds bands: The Mekons, Chumbawamba, Cyanide Pills, Gang of Four, Abrasive Wheels, The Wedding Present, Kaiser Chiefs, and Yard Act commanding my turntable at home, and Spotify elsewhere. Even The Smiths' 'Panic' played with its uncannily appropriate hail, 'The Leeds side-streets that you slip down. I wonder to myself'. As do I! Will we survive? Soothing sounds in a time of distress.

The second go-to was clichés shared on social media. I collected little snippets of text such as, 'Proud When We Win, Loyal When We Lose'; 'It's Not Just A Game, It's Our Life!'; 'We All Love Leeds Regardless'; 'Leeds Until I Die'; 'Win or Lose We Are Marching On Together'; 'Win, Lose, Draw, Or even get relegated, Always and

Forever Leeds'; 'It's not just 90 minutes, it's a lifetime'; 'Premier League or League 1, I don't give a toss'; 'Always Leeds and Proud MOT ALAW'. Though the term cliché has a negative ring to it, a novel expression become worn out from repetition, I found myself drawn to platitude.

In times of crisis, such clichés aren't tepid or stale remarks. The insipid becomes inspiring. They embolden, a show of solidarity in resistance to desperation. They do the work of my playlist: engulf the senses in hope, alliance, and closeness. They remind that a club, *this* club, is far more than a result, or a position in the league table; more than its owners, shareholders, managers and players. Nice when these actors align but they are transient in nature, only we remain, only we persevere. I don't ignore the financial repercussions of relegation: the depletion of a squad, inability to attract talent, possible loss of investors and sponsors, brand depreciation, stadia improvements indefinitely on-hold, forfeiture of lucrative media deals. The list is long and complex.

Still, I refuse to reduce football to financial matters. It must be more than money. It's about a city, whose pride in the club is witnessed in its murals joining the ranks of those in Derry, Mexico City, and Los Angeles. Public symbols of pride, unity, and identity. It's about club history, the present, and unwritten future – all verses in the epic that is Leeds United Football Club. It's about people who see and know themselves as Leeds no matter where. It's about community, togetherness, belonging, being, and feeling Leeds: the ups *and* downs.

Today, 11 May, after losing to Chelsea, in another 'must-win' match, I stare at the remaining fixtures on my laptop, hoping that they will reveal a secret to our safety. 'Can we get three points from Brighton on Sunday?' 'Who will score?' 'Will Gelhardt start?' Such questions are murmured quietly to myself. Not exactly an easy match with Brighton recently besting the likes of Spurs, Manchester United, and Arsenal. I do math, fetishising results, points dropped, of course, by Everton and Burnley. 'How about against Brentford away on the final day?' They beat Chelsea when we could not. A fluke? And they defeated Southampton when we could only draw. 'Will 40 points, the maximum we can achieve, be enough?' Brentford, 13th in the league table, eight points from the relegation zone where we reside on this day with Everton and Burnley both having 'games in hand'. I've truly learned to loathe that phrase this season, the sound of an injured animal in need of being put down for its own sake, release from its agonising pain.

Yet deafening love for Leeds United rings out around Elland Road and at every away ground. We're 3-0 down against Chelsea on 11 May and all I can hear is 'We All Love Leeds'. I turned up the television's volume to drown out my own feelings of sorrow.

No boos echo around Elland Road.

No player targeted for abuse.

No banners high with the word 'OUT' in all caps.

Although the commentator spoke of Leeds fans departing, I saw nothing but bodies twirling scarfs and singing together, to the end. Hope. Passion. Commitment. Loyalty. Love. That scene will stay with many no matter what league we play in next season, or the next. Supporting a club exceeds results, regardless of good or bad. Football, as Simon Critchley reminds us, is 'a theatre of identity – family, tribe, city, nation'. To this, I would add globe. Other Leeds fans the world over no doubt cranked up their television, mobile, or computer volume to feel the love at their location. We All Love Leeds unconditionally.

Today, 15 May, no red cards: three yellow cards picked up to make it a Premier League record; 100 in total, Dirty Leeds. Fifteen goal attempts, five on target against Brighton; compared to zero shots on target against Chelsea, and only two shots on target against Arsenal. Better play, more commitment and heart from the players. Going into the final ten minutes at 1-0 down against Brighton I start to think of Burnley's Thursday match against Aston Villa with Spurs already doing us a favour earlier this morning. They (and Everton) have it harder with the extra midweek matches, I console myself. We are truly in 'need-a-miracle' stage, now. Our faith not in our own hands (unless we gain points).

Again, *always*, the supporters at Elland Road, along with those watching loyally from afar, show their conviction and solidarity; singing their hearts out with anthems of togetherness, 'We Are Leeds', 'We All Love Leeds', 'All Leeds Aren't We', and the unfeigned battle cry, 'Marching On Together', which expresses so much zeal, rapport, and rapture in this moment. Into stoppage time: five calm, composed touches by Joe Gelhardt to best two Brighton defenders, the sixth, a cleverly calculated chip – over Lewis Dunk – to the back post met by the puissant head of Pascal Struijk who, just minutes after coming on as a substitute, was on the ground due to a head injury. The ball slipped past three defenders, just inside the post to cross the line. We equalised! Elation! A point celebrated raucously like a victory, in fact it was: enough to lift us out of the relegation zone, a lifeline to go again next Sunday: the lemon next to the pie. After my streaming concludes, I quickly switch to the club's official Facebook page to watch the players – those out due to injuries and suspensions as well – walk the pitch to applaud the supporters, beaming with hope, excitement, relief. Never easy with Leeds. All eyes now on Thursday.

Today, 19 May, Everton come from behind to beat Crystal Palace 3-2. They are safe and will not be relegated this season. Burnley pull off the unthinkable (in my mind at least): they draw 1-1 away to Aston Villa. Their goalkeeper, Nick Pope, in performance-of-the-season form. We are back in the relegation zone on goal difference.

Today, 21 May, eve of destruction or salvation? I am restless, cannot sleep. I battle my duvet with flailing limbs. My mood goes sombre, quiet. Cannot shake the dead-man-walking sensation no matter how hard I try. I want to believe, badly.

Today, 22 May, Big Sunday. Last day of the 2021/2022 Premier League season. Last win, 9 April against relegated

Watford. 'Bamford tests positive for Covid' is the news that greets my waking eyes. He is living life under a persistent dark cloud this season. No let-up. High blood pressure meds gulped down. The starting 11: Ilan Meslier, Junior Firpo, Robin Koch, Liam Cooper, Diego Llorente, Kalvin Phillips, Jack Harrison, Rodrigo, Raphinha, Sam Greenwood, Jack Gelhardt. On the bench: Kristoffer Klaesson, Pascal Struijk, Leo Fuhr Hjelde, Charlie Cresswell, Jamie Shackleton, Lewis Bate, Mateusz Klich, Archie Gray, and Tyler Roberts. Attack-minded start. Defensive bench. Names that will be remembered one way or another. Some perhaps playing their last game for us. Fortune smiles: Newcastle defeat Burnley 2-1. We defeat Brentford 2-1. We stay up, Burnley go down. We didn't start strong, our passing was poor, we had a goal disallowed, our defence remains porous, and another questionable substitution transpired (taking Gelhardt off instead of Rodrigo!?). Still, we won, and survived. Raphinha provides a possible parting gift in the form of a penalty won and converted. Harrison smashes home in stoppage time to clinch the winner. Tears. Emotions bottled up over the month of May – if not all season – pour out, uncontrollably. Solace, for now. Let's get it right next season. Make us believe Marsch!

I must admit that I was preparing myself for scenes of misery: a camera close-up on a young supporter crying, an older man shedding tears into his scarf. Supporters clapping the players. Players fighting back tears in their salute to the fans for their unflinching backing. Commentators playing the ventriloquist dummy, mouthing prefab scripts about: exhaustion, casualties of 'murderball', injuries, recruitment, being 'found out', and, most noxious, where Phillips and Raphinha, among others, will play next season. By stroke of luck, obstinance or some combination thereof, we were spared from such scenes.

After the 2021/22 season, I head to another beach, the west coast of Costa Rica, ready to once again dig my heel into untapped sand. The usual routine will unfold: the letters L-E-E-D-S-U-N-I-T-E-D impermanently drawn on to a beach with my Leeds beach towel sprawled out like a conquering flag, accompanied by my bottle opener popping off caps to the tune of 'Marching On Together'. And it's likely that Deck will slap stickers on unsuspecting surfaces at San José's Aeropuerto Internacional Juan Santamaria. I will plan my autumn, winter, and spring based upon next season's fixtures. Anticipating home matches in either October or November when Deck's school and my university calendar permits – possibly squeeze in a March visit pending our budget. Deck's scrapbook will expand, adding new ticket stubs, photos, and newspaper clippings. I will buy him a new kit in time for his annual autumn school photo like always. Old enamel badges will be affixed on new lapels. Club memberships renewed before the final whistle blew on the current season. We are Leeds.

Bibliography

Ahmed, S., *Queer Phenomenology: Orientations, Objects, Others* (Durham, NC: Duke University Press, 2006)

BBC Match of the Day: Leeds United (1992, BBC Enterprises Ltd, videocassette)

Benjamin, W., 'Paris, Capital of the Nineteenth Century', *Reflections: Essays, Aphorisms, Autobiographical Writing* (Trans. Edmund Jephcott, New York: Schocken Books, 1986)

'Bouncing Babies'. The Teardrop Explodes (MCA/Razz Records, 1981, vinyl)

Bowie, D., 'Queen Bitch', *Honky Dory* (RCA Victor, 1971, vinyl)

Castile, M., *Driver's License* (London: Bloomsbury Academic, 2014)

Claude: P., *Football Disco!: The Unbelievable World of Football Record Covers* (Koln: Konig, 2019)

Coles, S., *The Anatomy of Type* (New York: Harper Design, 2012)

Connon, S., *Paraphernalia: The Curious Lives of Magical Things* (London: Profile Books, 2011)

Critchley, S., *What We Think About When We Think About Football* (London: Profile Books, 2017)

Eisenberg, Evan., *The Recording Angel* (New Haven, Yale University Press, 1987)

Felski, R., *Hooked: Art and Attachment* (Chicago: University of Chicago Press, 2020)

'FIFA 20 Decides!', Facebook, 15 March 2020 (Available online: https://www.facebook.com/watch/LeedsUnited/277228813274004/)

Glanville, B., *The Footballer's Companion* (London: Eyre & Spottiswoode, 1962)

Gray, D., *Black Boots & Football Pinks: 50 Lost Wonders Of The Beautiful Game* (London: Bloomsbury, 2018)

Harrison, T., *V* (Hexham, Bloodaxe Books, 1985)

Hine, T., *The Total Package: The Secret History and Hidden Meanings of Boxes, Bottles, Cans, and Other Persuasive Containers* (Boston: Back Bay Books, 1995)

Hoggart, R., *The Uses of Literacy* (London: Penguin, 1956)

Hooper, T., (director) *The Damned United* (Columbia Pictures, BBC Films, 2009)

Hornby, N., *Fever Pitch* (New York: Riverhead Books, 1992)

Hornby, N., *High Fidelity* (London: Penguin, 1995)

Knausgaard, K.O., and Ekelund, F., *Home and Away: Writing The Beautiful Game* (New York: Farrar, Straus and Giroux, 2017)

Leach, S., *Twenty Football Towns* (Salford: Saraband, 2020)

Leeds United Football Team, 'Leeds, Leeds, Leeds', *Leeds United* (Chapter 1, 1972, vinyl)

Leeds United's Greatest FA Cup Victories (1991, Watershed Pictures, videocassette)

Leeds United's Race For The Title 1989/90 (1990, Castle Vision, videocassette)

Lowry, L.S., *Going to the Match* (painting, 1953)

MacInnes, P., 'Digital Fans Represent Football's Future So Should Clubs Start Listening?' *The Guardian*, 19 January 2022

McLuhan, M., *Understanding Media: The Extensions of Man* (New York: Signet, 1964)

Orange Juice, 'Rip It Up', *Rip It Up* (Polydor, 1982, vinyl)

Orwell, G., 'The Moon Under Water', *Evening Standard*, 9 February 1946

Plenderleith, I., *The Quiet Fan* (London: Unbound, 2018)

Riach, J., 'Marcelo Bielsa transformed Leeds with decency, humility, and hard work', *The Guardian*, 27 February 2022

Rickson, T., *Football Is Better With Fans* (Worthing: Pitch Publishing, 2021)

Robinson, J., and Jonathan, C., *The Club: How The English Premier League Became The Wildest, Richest, Most Disruptive Force in Sports* (Boston: Houghton and Mifflin Harcourt, 2018)

Rostron, P., *We Are The Damned United: The Real Story of Brian Clough at Leeds United* (Edinburgh: Mainstream Publishing Co., 2009)

Russo, A., and Russo, J., *Avengers: Infinity War* (Marvel Studios, Walt Disney Pictures, 2018)

Scott, A.O., 'A Soccer Coach Divides and Doesn't Conquer', *New York Times*, 8 October 2009

Sharpe, G., *Vinyl Countdown* (Herts: Oldcastle Books, 2019)

Sievey, C., and The Freshies, 'If You Really Love Me Buy Me A Shirt', *If You Really Love Me Buy Me A Shirt* (CV Songs, 1981, vinyl)

Simons, E., *The Secret Lives of Sports Fans: The Science of Obsession* (New York: Overlook Duckworth, 2013)

Spitznagel, E., *Old Records Never Die* (New York: Plume, 2016)

Stewart, K., *Ordinary Affects* (Durham: NC: Duke University Press, 2007)

The Clash, 'I'm So Bored With The USA', *The Clash* (CBS, 1977, vinyl)

The Crew, 'Leeds, Leeds, Leeds (Marching On Together)', *Leeds, Leeds, Leeds (Marching On Together)* (Q Music, 1992, vinyl)

The Exploited, 'Fuck The USA', *Troops of Tomorrow* (Secret Records, 1982, vinyl)

The Freshies, 'I Can't Get "Bouncing Babies" By The Teardrop Explodes', *I Can't Get*

The Undertones, 'My Perfect Cousin', *My Perfect Cousin* (Sire, 1980, vinyl)

The 1991-1992 Season: Leeds United The Champions (1992, Polygram Video Ltd, videocassette)

The 1992 Tennents F.A. Charity Shield: Leeds United v Liverpool (1992, Watershed Pictures Production, videocassette)

Thompson, E.P., 'Review of *The Long Revolution* Part I & II', *New Left Review*, 9 & 10, 1961

Turkle, S., *Evocative Objects: Things We Think With* (Cambridge, MA: MIT Press, 2007)

YorkshireSquare. 'Adjusting to Life as a "Widow of Bielsa",' *Marching On Together*, 28 February 2022

1972 FA Cup Final: Leeds United v Arsenal (1990, BBC Enterprises Ltd, videocassette)